RUN TO THE FIRE

FAGAN'S WAY

Chris McLeod and Sam Harvey

Published by Wilkinson Publishing Pty Ltd
ACN 006 042 173
PO Box 24135, Melbourne, VIC 3001, Australia.
Ph: +61 3 9654 5446
enquiries@wilkinsonpublishing.com.au
www.wilkinsonpublishing.com.au

WilkinsonPublishing
wilkinsonpublishinghouse

A catalogue record of this book is available from the National Library of Australia.
ISBN: 9781921667176

Cover design: Michael Bannenberg.
Cover image Mark Stewart, Newspix. Altered by Firefly AI.

Printed and bound in Australia by Ligare.

CONTENTS

RUN TO THE FIRE

Brisbane's 2025 back-to-back premiership wasn't exactly a walk in the park, despite the Grand Final scoreline indicating that a 47-points victory might have been an emphatic end to the season.

What is remarkable is that Brisbane under Chris Fagan had risen from the wooden spoon when he took over as coach almost a decade ago to reach three Grand Finals in a row and collect two premierships.

It is even more remarkable that Chris Fagan took a short leave of absence in 2022 during the Hawthorn racism saga and even thought about walking away from the game mid-season back in 2024, such were the pressures he felt during the AFL racism saga and dealing with his own health concerns.

It was always going to be difficult in 2025 for the Lions to repeat the performance of the previous year, a 60-point victory over the more-fancied Sydney Swans. A year later and the Lions had an even tougher fixture list and more injuries to contend with.

At the start of the 2025 season, a fair proportion of fans (25% according to an AFL survey) liked the Lions' chances of a repeat premiership.

They finished third on the ladder after their last home-and-away game, on Sunday 24 August, with 17 wins and six losses.

As the September finals series started, the Adelaide Crows were considered "most likely." They sat on top of the ladder (18 wins, five losses) and their prospects looked even more promising after the Lions lost to Geelong at the MCG in the Qualifying Final.

Revenge on Geelong, at the MCG three weeks later, was going to be sweet.

Brisbane opened its AFL premiership defence in 2025 on the SCG against Sydney with a dramatic four-point victory over the home team. Chris Fagan ranked it among the club's great wins given the obstacles to be overcome.

The Lions were four goals down before scoring a major of their own. They took control but had to withstand a final-quarter fightback by the Swans, the opponents they had crushed by 10 goals in the 2024 Grand Final five months earlier.

Brisbane finished without a couple of key players: Charlie Cameron was a late withdrawal because of a calf strain, Kai Lohmann (ankle) was substituted early, and Brandon Starcevich suffered a concussion in the fourth quarter.

Cameron's absence opened the gate for 18-year-old Levi Ashcroft to make his AFL debut alongside his brother Will in the Lions line-up.

Chris Fagan addressed the new boy in the final training run before the season-opener: "It is a bloody fair effort to break into this side when you think of it.

"Of the 23 that represented this club in the Grand Final last year, the only bloke missing is Joey (Joe Daniher) because he retired, but everybody is fit and available for selection.

"So on the back of having shoulder surgery, a bit of a later start to the pre-season, then getting involved in some of the later practice games, you've been able to force your way into the side which is a remarkable effort when you think about it.

"We wish you all the best, continue the Ashcroft tradition in the Brisbane Lions family and play alongside your brother (Will) which is going to be really exciting.

"We know you are going to make a huge contribution to the team when you come onto the ground, so well done."

Levi didn't disappoint; the young midfielder collected 25 possessions, had four clearances and six score involvements.

The other AFL coaches over the previous two years had seen how Chris Fagan was able to inspire his team in big matches. They would create ways of dealing with the strength of the Lions – or at least should have.

Fagan would have known his methods were becoming familiar and he would have to devise a new way of motivating his players.

One thing that had worked for him was to adopt a mantra that instilled in players what was expected of them in the face of adversity.

In 2024 after a Round 22 loss at the Gabba that cost them a top-four spot after rising from the bottom four, Fagan told his players: "If you're walking on thin ice, you may as well dance."

And dance the Lions did, all the way to their first premiership in two decades, becoming only the second team from the bottom four of the top-eight to win the premiership since the finals format changed in 2000.

How could he get his players in 2025 to believe in themselves and win again?

The banner held aloft as the team – the underdogs if the pundits were to be believed – ran on to the MCG on Saturday 27 September said it all in a single word: "Believe"

The path to the "big dance" hadn't been easy, with a small

amount of comfort to be had from winning the previous year. The tough draw and significant injury challenges plagued Fagan all season.

At times, the Lions struggled, even against middle-rung teams. Their schedule was among the most difficult of all teams – they played five top-nine opponents twice and only the bottom-three teams once.

They also had to deal with three five-day breaks during the season that proved physically demanding and put players under stress as they backed up in short turnarounds. Losses against teams lower on the ladder and a costly draw with North Melbourne all added to the pressure later in the season.

What was Fagan going to do to inspire his team?

At the suggestion of Jarrod Berry who had heard a boxing trainer tell his charge, "Run towards the fire," Chris Fagan adopted the epithet to spur the Lions. He even hung a fireman's helmet on a wall of the clubrooms and turned to it whenever he needed to get something special from the players.

It hit a note with the Lions as they overcame a mounting injury list and difficult draw to go all the way, again.

"It all started in round 15 when we played Geelong in Geelong," co-captain Harris Andrews recalled.

"We lost to the Giants the week before and we felt like we played a bit safe at times when the stakes were really high.

"So, from that moment on, we just wanted to run towards the fire. No matter what happened.

"We had a fireman come in and talk about what it was like actually running into a fire and all the things that go into that.

"It is all just a testament to 'Fages' as a coach because it was a great theme which really worked for us.

"He is always looking for ways to motivate and inspire us, and he did it again.

"Put the helmet on, buckle up, and get in there."

Perhaps there was also some influence from the TV show *Chicago Fire*, and the words of character Kelly Severide, played by Taylor Kinnery: "You know what we do. We run toward the fire."

According to Jay Clark in the *Herald Sun*, the fire-fighting inspiration for the Lions originated with long-time fan and first-class firefighter, Mick Brumley, from Cannon Hill fire station 7.

Clark: "Brumley would pick up his morning coffee from the same Brisbane cafe as Fagan.

"And one morning when the pair were talking by chance, the senior coach asked if Brumley and his station officer, Justin Francis, could speak to his players about the dangers of their day jobs.

"And Brumley donated a spare white helmet so it could go on the road with the Lions."

Brumley told Clark: "I was sitting there looking at them (players) thinking they are my heroes and they are looking back at me (in a similar way), so it really was a great honour.

"I am generally on the hose, and I go into the buildings and that sort of thing, but I rely on the people in my team to help look after me.

"Whether it is the pump operator so I have got water, or making sure I'm out (of the building) before I run out of air.

"That teamwork is what I spoke about and how we deal with adversity, looking after each other and relying on our training.

"They (Lions) asked me 'What do you do when you are faced

with a dangerous situation?' You look at your team members.

"One time there was a guy lying on a powerline and I thought, 'If I get electrocuted here these guys should be able to bring me back' (to life).

"So we have got a close crew. The camaraderie is strong.

"And there are some similarities (to football), I guess."

The record shows the Lions responded in the best way possible. Whatever the level of inspiration, the words captured the mindset that was needed to face challenges and confront them head-on.

The Lions moved into second place in Round 15 after defeating Geelong and stayed there until slipping to third after Round 21 and a big loss to the Gold Coast. They didn't fall below third for the rest of the season.

Chris Fagan explained: "We would put Mick's helmet up in the rooms.

"You are always looking for things to help motivate the players and that definitely helped us because the win over Geelong in Geelong was a really important win in our season.

"So we just kept it going.

"We had a lot of challenges this year, we had six or seven new players compared to last year's grand final, so it is a massive turnover.

"But I said to the boys, 'You are like cockroaches. You can't kill us'."

Fagan's approach is often credited with inspiring loyalty and determination among his players, reinforcing his reputation as a coach who builds strong relationships and positive team culture.

Those thoughts were put aside in the lead-up to Grand

Final day; the pundits (and punters) were warming to the Geelong Cats, a team that well remembered how Brisbane ended their season in the Preliminary Final in 2024. And they'd put Brisbane to the sword three weeks previously in the Qualifying Final.

Even with the Grand Final scores level at the main break, 5.6 (36) apiece, Geelong was still looking "the goods."

At halftime, Fagan's message focussed on resetting, emphasising resilience, and treating the second half as a fresh start with the scoreboard "back to zero."

That was a throwback to 2024 when he told his players "Be like a goldfish" – forget what's happened so far, move on.

He urged his players to knuckle down, maintain composure, and repeat the strong basics that had kept them even with Geelong to that point.

A coach can't play the game for his team. He can mastermind tactics, but often it will be his words that hit home with the players when they need inspiration.

And that's a strength of Chris Fagan.

Team insiders described his half-time speech as practical and calm. Typical. The message got through. The Lions' explosive third-quarter surge blew the Cats away and secured the Lions a back-to-back premiership.

Fagan had encouraged the team to "take risks" and play with confidence.

As well, he had a trump card up his sleeve. He gambled by putting his recovering co-captain Lachie Neale on the bench until half-time. You could see the players' faces brighten as Neale ran out with them to start the assault on the Cats.

There was the inspiration, there and then.

The man who many thought had gone for the season with a calf injury was to play a crucial role in securing the Lions' victory.

Neale's contribution in just one quarter: seven disposals, seven clearances and a pivotal goal.

By the time the final sire sounded, the Lions had run to the fire... and extinguished it.

Brisbane Lions 18-14 (122)

Geelong Cats 11-9 (75)

Fans may not have wanted to get ahead of themselves yet, but many of them would have already been thinking about a three-peat in 2026.

They'd danced on thin ice in 2024 and run to the fire in 2025. What would 2026 bring?

CASE FOR THE DEFENCE

The question: how would the Lions in 2025 back up after their stunning victory over the Sydney Swans in the 2024 Grand Final?

Things didn't go well as their title defence began. Cyclone Alfred rubbed out their scheduled Opening Round game at home against Geelong when they would have unfurled the premiership flag before their horde of loyal supporters.

The first game then became a visit to Sydney for a Grand Final rematch in Round 1. To top it off, Chris Fagan was unable to name a full-strength team to start the game and had to deal with some injury setbacks as it progressed.

All that was put to one side as the Lions found a way to snatch a four-point victory over the hosts and lay to rest thoughts they might be suffering a Grand Final hangover.

Their first home game for the year a week later had fans on edge early, but the Lions prevailed over the West Coast Eagles for a second come-from-behind victory.

Cyclone Alfred had blown itself out when Brisbane at last got to play their Opening Round clash against the Geelong Cats at the Gabba in what should have been a Round 3 bye. But it was still raining.

The weather and venue were different, but there were similarities to their Preliminary Final clash at the MCG back in September 2024.

Then, Geelong had a 19-point lead but by three-quarter time Brisbane led by two and went on to win by 10.

In the March 2025 clash, the Cats led by 32 points in the second term and 26 points at the main break. The Lions conjured a 28-point turn-around to lead by a point at the final change and went on to win by 11 points.

Was it a Ted Lasso (fictional TV football coach) moment from Chris Fagan at half-time – "be a goldfish" – or was it the drying out of the ground in the second half that kicked the Lions into gear for their third victory of the season and another come-from-behind performance?

The Lions followed that up with a tight win over Richmond then went 5-0 and at the top of the ladder with yet another come-from-behind win, over the Bulldogs in Adelaide for Gather Round on12 April.

It was the Lions' first 5-0 start to a season in 77 years. The 60-point second-half turnaround was also the fourth time the Lions had come from behind to win. The exception was the Richmond game where the Lions led at every change.

The comeback trend started in 2024 in Round 16 against Melbourne and continued through the finals series with tough wins away over GWS and Geelong, the Lions having trailed by big margins in both matches.

Lions fans were well pleased to see their team set the early-season pace in 2025, even if they faced the toughest imaginable draw in the run home.

And there were some injuries. In the back of the minds of some followers there remained concerns about a premiership hangover.

Much was to happen before the end of season 2025, and much would test the resilience of Fagan, his players, and supporters.

But lionhearted was still very much an appropriate word, just as it was as Chris Fagan rebuilt the team over the years after his appointment in 2016.

'We never win. We never lose. We either win or we learn'

Lifelong Lions supporter SAM HARVEY picks up the story.

Backing up a premiership-winning season is never straightforward. Climbing the mountain once is a daunting feat – but scaling it again, knowing the physical and mental toll it demands, is exquisitely arduous.

History tells us that post-premiership hangovers are real. Success, while exhilarating, can also be disorienting. Across the sporting world, there are cautionary tales of teams whose championship highs were followed by unexpected lows. Manchester City, now a modern football juggernaut, were relegated from England's topflight in 1937/38 – just one season after lifting the First Division title. It remains the only instance of a reigning English champion being relegated the very next year.

In the NBA, the Miami Heat endured a similarly sobering comedown. After winning the 2006/07 championship, they slumped to a 15–67 record the following season – the worst in franchise history – battling injuries and key player retirements in what became a season to forget.

Back home, the AFL has had its fair share of premiership deflations. Since 1990, eight reigning premiers have failed to reach the finals the following year: Collingwood (1991), Essendon (1994), Adelaide (1999), Hawthorn (2009), the Western Bulldogs (2017), Richmond (2021), Geelong (2023), and again, Collingwood in 2024. For both Adelaide and Richmond, the drop came after consecutive flags – with Adelaide plummeting to 13th in 1999, marking the steepest fall from premiership glory on record.

It seems that in elite sport, reaching the summit is hard – staying there can be even harder.

Fages was adamant post-win in the 2024 Grand Final that there was still unfinished business.

Speaking with esteemed journalist Michael Whiting for AFL.com.au, Fages spoke about the clear message for 2025…

"… a lot of people will want to talk to you about the success you've just had, and it will become intoxicating," Fagan said.

"In its worst form you might develop a sense of entitlement, and the best way to handle a Grand Final win is to be humble and respectful to everybody and not get carried away.

"I think there's a confidence you can get from winning a premiership because you know the way you play and the players you've got are good enough."

This clear message had a profound effect on the playing group as the previous two Grand Final victors in Geelong (2022) and Collingwood (2023) both missed the finals the following year. Fages didn't want the group to make that same mistake.

"If you remain humble and hard-working then the rest should

take care of itself," he said.

With 11 team members playing a league record 27 games in a season (all teams played 23 home-and-away games instead of 22 in 2024 due to Gather Round), it was paramount that the boys rested and recovered after a gruelling 2024 finals campaign.

The 2025 season proved to be our (the Lions') toughest challenge so far. Our descent back into regular-season reality was anything but gentle. Injuries mounted, the fixture was unforgiving, and form ebbed and flowed like a typical Queensland summer storm. And yet, somehow, we emerged from the chaos in third place on the ladder, securing another shot at glory.

Our final win of the home-and-away season – a gritty 10-point victory over Hawthorn in Round 24 – sealed our place in the top four. It marked the fifth time we'd finished in the top four during Chris Fagan's nine seasons at the helm, earning us the coveted double chance in September. Fagan called it our "best ever" home-and-away campaign – not for dominance, but for resilience.

"This one means more," he admitted post-match. *"It's been a high degree of difficulty."*

And he wasn't wrong. At times, our injury list resembled a triage ward. Key players such as Jack Payne, Noah Answerth, Keidean Coleman, and Lincoln McCarthy spent significant time sidelined. Later, the absences of Lachie Neale, Jarrod Berry, and Eric Hipwood further stretched our depth. Meanwhile, the fixture offered little relief. We faced double-ups against the powerhouses that are Collingwood and Geelong, and a resurgent Gold Coast Suns outfit playing their best footy to date.

There were moments when our premiership defence appeared on the brink. A heavy loss in the Q-Clash, followed by a two-point defeat to Sydney in Round 22, saw us drop to fifth – a position not unfamiliar, having finished there in 2024. With a backline held together by tape, the season made for some nervous viewing. Unlike 2023 and 2024, we weren't blowing teams away.

Our percentage was the lowest of any top-nine side – a reflection of our inconsistencies and injuries. Yet our record against quality opposition was elite: seven wins from 12 games against top-eight teams. We knocked over Collingwood and Hawthorn at the MCG, and Geelong at GMHBA Stadium – all by four or more goals. Each of those sides would go on to reach the preliminary finals.

When it mattered most, we stood up.

"There's an honesty piece with Brisbane that I really like," said SEN commentator and 2018 premiership coach Adam Simpson on 31 July.

"They might not win the flag, but if they do, it would be one of the better achievements that I've seen."

A recurring theme in 2025 was our ability to rise as the stakes increased. Time and again, when adversity struck, we responded. Following a disappointing home loss to Sydney – a game in which we only came alive in the final five minutes – we bounced back with a gutsy win over Fremantle in Perth, then followed up with a determined victory over Hawthorn.

Fagan, almost humouring the inaccuracy, praised the composure shown despite kicking 11.23.

"I've seen teams kick like that and lose," he said. *"We didn't. We stayed positive."*

That positivity – from both coach and fans – was tested all year. Not just by injuries, but by the burden of being the hunted.

As Fagan put it: *"Everyone picks your game to pieces when you win a flag."*

The Lions didn't always look like world-beaters, but we looked like survivors, galvanised by Fagan, and sometimes that's an even harder thing to be.

Resilience over adversity

If you were a Lions fan in 2025, you probably still get a twitch thinking about the season. It wasn't exactly smooth sailing – more like up s**t creek without a paddle. Injuries piled up, form slipped away, and every second article seemed to predict our downfall before the siren had even sounded.

I didn't want to use injuries as an excuse if we weren't to reach the zenith. There were other clubs with injury lists that exceeded ours. Essendon, for example, played 44 different players in 2025 and blooded 15 debutants. We just seemed to get untimely injuries when it appeared we could least afford them. Even a couple of days after our gutsy Preliminary Final win against the Magpies, we still didn't know if our beloved co-captain and star, Lachie Neale, was going to play.

Every morning, Dad would grab the paper from the footpath out the front of our place – still old-school like that – and read out the latest piece about "cracks in the armour" or "reasons Brisbane can't go deep in finals." We'd roll our eyes; Dad would have a sip of his tea and remind us that the media's job is to panic first and think later.

But here's the thing – every week, somehow, the boys

bounced back. Players went down, game plans shifted, and yet we found a way to stay in the fight.

Word got around that during the bye Fages and the coaching staff had drawn up a whole new game style, just in case teams figured it out and put plans in place to counter our usual ones. It wouldn't have shocked anyone that he ended up nabbing the AFL Coach of the Year for a record third time. That man could probably organise a premiership tilt from a backyard kick-to-kick.

From the stands at the Gabba, to the 'G, Marvel, down the highway in Geelong, Norwood Oval, at the pub with mates, or curled up on the couch while the rain hammered against the windows (classic Melbourne weekend), it all started to feel like something bigger than wins and losses. It was about hanging on – about seeing what we were really made of.

As the season progressed, it seemed that the higher the stakes were, the better we played. That became a little frustrating as we dropped winnable games yet always managed to find an answer the following week.

There were many moments that stood out during the year.

Games such as our second-half domination against the Bulldogs at Norwood Oval – we came back from 39 points down to kick 15.7 (97), or our blistering first quarter against Port Adelaide in Round 17, when we kicked 8.4 (52) including seven goals in 17 minutes of footy.

We had the ability to flick the switch and produce the best footy played all year, kicking five or more goals in any given period of time with ease, which meant that even if we weren't Top 4, the rest of the teams were wary of us as it wasn't out of the realm of possibility that we could win a Premiership from anywhere in the eight.

Our ability to win on the road became one of the defining motifs of the season; a travelling side producing one of the most remarkable away records in recent memory. Fifteen games interstate in 2025 yielded an 11–1–3 return. Remove the 66-point stumble at Carrara, and the ledger becomes even more striking: 11–1–2, the strongest interstate performance by any club since West Coast dominated the highways and airways in 1991 and 2006. Those wins, collected in hostile territory, under foreign lights, became the one of the season's great storylines.

Round 11 took us to Melbourne, a familiar city but a daunting task: Hawthorn at the MCG, twilight on a Saturday, the Lions chasing down a 21-year hoodoo. The Hawks, sitting comfortably in fourth, had the look of a side ready to press its case. Yet the day began quietly, almost gently. I'd slipped down to Elsternwick Park to watch my sister Billie run out for her 50th, the soft winter sun lingering just long enough before I returned to Richmond and made my way to the MCG. The previous week's late fade-out against Melbourne still stung, and Fages' 200th loomed large. Confidence came in whispers – Tom, Dad and our mate Nick Little, each of us carrying a private hope the group would right its course.

And then the familiar script of this team re-emerged. A three-point deficit at the first break dissolved in a flurry of precision and audacity: seven goals in the space of one storming second quarter.

Charlie Cameron, whose form had flickered across the early part of the season, caught fire – three goals in three minutes, the kind of burst that resets an entire arena. From there the match tilted decisively. A 33-point victory felt fitting, almost poetic, for a coach marking his double-century against the club where he once served as the head of football operations under the Clarkson regime. In a quiet aside, the numbers told another story. Of the 200 games under Fages, Hugh McCluggage had played 193 of them, Dayne Zorko 187, Eric Hipwood 178, followed by Jarrod Berry (170) and Charlie Cameron (165) – the true constants of an era.

The road stretched south next, down the long curve of the Princes Highway to the Cattery, a venue that had a habit of turning even the most seasoned teams brittle (except for GWS!). Kardinia Park had not offered us a victory in 22 years, and its ghosts lingered. Two of those losses had been by a single point – one in 2013, when Ash McGrath's six goals nearly dragged us across the line before Ryan Lester's last desperate kick fell short; and the infamous 2021 night when Zac Bailey caught Mark Blicavs cold, only for umpire Rob O'Gorman to swallow the whistle. I'd watched that one on my phone at the Burleigh Pavilion (Qld), grimacing with every replay. Dad, who'd been in the stands that night surrounded by the enemy, never really recovered.

(It was the famous night of the COVID flight when a half-time announcement requested all Lions supporters that had flown in from Queensland to leave the ground immediately). In hindsight, they were able to avoid the horrible umpiring non-decision.

This time was different, even before the bounce. It was my first game in Geelong, and as we drove in on a soft Friday afternoon, the stakes seemed to thicken with every passing kilometre. Third on the ladder, two points clear of Adelaide and Hawthorn, but still feeling precarious. Jack Payne – our hero of the 2024 prelim – had ruptured his patella tendon. Darcy Gardiner was scratched late as we sat eating our chicken parmas at The Cremorne Hotel. The omens weren't kind.

But football often ignores omens.

Darcy Wilmot set the tone early, slicing through the middle for a running goal that carried the sort of energy you can't easily explain. Logan Morris announced himself the previous week with five goals and kicked five again, a performance that suggested that we had quietly begun grooming the heir to Joe Daniher's throne. Geelong's kicking was errant (6.15), but the real tale was in the spread. We pulled the Cats apart with our uncontested ball, a rare feat on their home patch.

A 41-point win felt less like an upset and more like a statement – a reminder to the competition that the reigning premiers had not, in fact, loosened their grip.

If 2024 was a season built on pleasant surprises, 2025 became the year of shedding burdens. Hoodoos dissolved one by one. The pressure of defending a premiership, the scrutiny from every corner of the football world, only sharpened our resolve. The win in Geelong in Round 15, paired with the Round 21 triumph over Collingwood, carried the weight of tests deliberately set – by media, by supporters, by rivals determined to measure our true steel. Those matches would take on new meaning later, when both opponents reappeared in September.

Beating a powerhouse during the home-and-away grind is one thing; beating them in a final, far from home, is another entirely. Having already broken the 22-year drought at Kardinia Park and the 21-year finals drought over Geelong the previous season, we wondered – almost nervously – whether the group had yet another charge left in it.

And so, as fate tends to enjoy circling back, Geelong awaited us once more – this time, under the sharp lights of a Qualifying Final.

The Cats were brutal in the first quarter, Jeremy Cameron was everywhere and got on top of Ryan Lester early with 7 kicks, 5 marks and 2.3. The boys were only two goals down, thanks to Geelong's woeful kicking in front of the big sticks. It felt like we were six goals down.

As seems to be the way in our clashes against the Cats there had to be a hero and a villain. Cam Rayner who was our Preliminary Final hero in 2024 with his left foot, turned into an anarchistic fire-starter sparking controversy with two pivotal free kicks and fiery celebrations. Despite his theatrics and a brief momentum swing, Geelong's versatility and composure helped them take control. In the end, Geelong's discipline and versatility powered them to a convincing win and yet another preliminary final appearance, defeating us by 38 points. To make matters worse our star co-captain and dual Brownlow Medallist Lachie Neale looked to have torn his calf and was visibly emotional on the interchange.

Fages gave his post-game opinion: *"It looks like he's done a calf, so that's not a good thing. He's a pretty tough sort of guy and can usually play through those but he couldn't, so I'm not expecting great news there... I don't know the severity because you need to get a scan to find out, but he's a pretty tough guy and it takes a lot for him to come off so I suspect it's something significant,"* he said.

"Do I think we can win the premiership (without Lachie)? I haven't even thought about that. I'm just worried about trying to win a game next week. I'll probably stay neutral on the answer to that question. I don't know.

"We'll continue to play with spirit and go at the game and get out there next week and try and deliver a better performance than we delivered tonight."

This meant that we would play the winner of Fremantle and Gold Coast in the Semi-Final the next week. Gold Coast who were playing in their first ever Final found a fitting hero as veteran David Swallow, who had been at the club since their birth and stayed loyal, kicked the match-winning point. Watching this game at the Richmond Club Hotel, I was filled with dread as this fairytale dream-like momentum the Suns had was all too similar to our 2024 campaign. The stage was set for a mouth-watering all-Queensland final at the Gabba.

Liam and I flew up Friday afternoon with Tom joining us in the evening. As is the way when arriving in Brisbane, we headed to the familiar Pineapple Hotel to watch Adelaide try to dodge the dreaded straight-sets tag against the brash and loud Hawthorn outfit. Witnessing Adelaide capitulate and get bounced out in straight-sets on home soil filled me with a glass-half-full approach reminding myself and Liam that at least if it did happen to us, it happened to Adelaide first. Liam and I are naturally glass-half-empty creatures, so it was great when Tommy linked up with us and fellow Lion Ben Zannoni joined to give us some much-needed reassurance.

Heading to the Pineapple pre-game we were amazed by

the contrast between Lions and Suns fans. Not only was The Pineapple 80% filled with Gold Coast supporters, they were yelling, dancing, singing and sculling their drinks, the complete opposite to the Lions fans at the pub, who were calm before the storm, albeit a little nervous, but locked in and ready for the game. We had been there before, witnessed the greatest, we knew what it took to get there.

Lose a soldier, replace with another soldier

Chris Fagan had to deal with some big issues in 2025, mainly involving injuries and an inexplicable – brief – loss of form by the Lions.

The squad's depth became important as injuries bit during the season.

July 2025 was a significant period that tested the resilience of the reigning premiers.

Round 21 pitted the Lions against the Collingwood Magpies in an MCG match to which the oft-used term "blockbuster" had been applied by the media.

The Lions did not have a great record against the Magpies, having lost their last four matches and hadn't beaten them at the MCG since 2014. Here they were, sitting third on the ladder and coming off a 66-point thrashing by Queensland neighbours the Golf Coast Suns the previous week.

Fagan was in no doubt about the seriousness of the situation:

We have to bounce back, no choice.

We were so disappointed the way that we played last week. It was a very un-Brisbane like performance, so as much as anything, we need to bounce back from that.

We're looking forward to the big occasion. A big crowd there. It's Collingwood.

They've had the wood on us the last four times that they've played us.

Of the loss to the Gold Coast: *It was a bit of a 'near enough is good enough' performance. And as it turned out, it was nowhere near good enough.*

We need to fix that up, and the leaders are a big part of that.

I will say this though, it's uncharacteristic. Don't make it sound like it's something that happens every week, it hasn't.

It's just a one-week thing. It better be a one-week thing.

The Magpies were premiers in 2023 but were struggling in 2024, eventually finishing 9th and missing the play-offs.

The Lions had some serious injury woes as they headed into the game.

Keidean Coleman was thought likely to be unavailable for the remainder of the season after the recurrence of a quad problem.

Conor McKenna (hamstring) and Kai Lohmann (calf) also looked unlikely to reappear before the end of the home-and-away season, and Jack Payne, Noah Answerth and Lincoln McCarthy had already finished their season.

Fagan: *Lose a soldier, replace them with another soldier. That's the mindset.*

We had those issues last year. We've been doing it this year too. These things happen.

It's a bit of a blow to our stocks, but it's a marathon, and different things pop up at different times.

What it does is creates opportunities for others to come in and play well. That's what happened last year when we look back, we had an injury crisis, and we identified some players that ended up being pretty good players for us.

The Lions bounced back in no uncertain terms, leading at every break, and holding off a second-term surge and defeating Collingwood 14.8 (92) to 10.5 (65).

Second-year player Logan Morris bagged a career-high six goals, as the replacement "soldiers" of emerging stars and wise heads stepped up for the visiting team to stamp its name on a double-chance place in the looming finals series.

Zac Bailey sealed the game with just over three-and a-half-minutes to play.

The injury toll continued to mount. Lions defender Ryan Lester was subbed out with concussion before quarter time.

No one was more impressed with the bounce-back than Chris Fagan who told Fox Footy afterwards: *(That was) definitely one of the better wins I've been involved with since I've been at the club.*

I loved the way we attacked the game tonight, we played bold footy... every time that they came at us, we were able to respond and stay steady.

It was a timely win helping set up the Lions for a double-shot chance in the finals series.

The Lions lost only one more game in the home-and-away series, to Hawthorn by 10 points, and defeating Sydney by two and Fremantle by 57 to finish third.

The Lions didn't start the finals series well, losing to Geelong then the Gold Coast Suns again, but ending Collingwood's finals run with a 29-point victory in the preliminary final for a shot at back-to-back premierships against Geelong.

A TOUCH OF GENIUS

Chris Fagan gambled by naming Lachie Neale as his "tactical substitute" player in the Grand Final. Twice a Brownlow medallist and a premiership player in 2024, Neale missed the last three games of the 2025 home-and-away series with a quad injury.

He was thought likely to be gone until the next season. Then there was good news – he would be back for the finals.

But there was more bad news. Another injury at the start of the finals meant he most likely would not play in the Grand Final.

Co-captain Neale was a crucial cog in the Lions' successful midfield machine and had been so since arriving from Fremantle at the end of 2018.

He missed seven games in 2021 with back and ankle problems. Until injured in 2025, he'd missed just eight of the Lions' 165 matches.

Neale was always going to figure in the Lions' quest for back-to-back premierships.

He was a star in Brisbane's 27-point win over Collingwood at the MCG in Round 21 on 2 August, with 36 disposals (12 clearances). But he reported soreness afterwards.

Scans revealed a quad tear that would sideline him until the finals.

At the time, Brisbane was third on the ladder and needed to

win just one of its three remaining games to guarantee a place in the play-offs. That didn't seem like an impossible ask, but the injuries were adding up.

Already on the club's "out" list were Jack Payne, Noah Answerth, Lincoln McCarthy and Keidean Coleman, their season over. Kai Lohmann (calf), Conor McKenna (hamstring) and Ryan Lester (concussion) also had injuries that threatened to derail their hopes of finals football.

Neale reappeared for the qualifying final against Geelong at the MCG on 5 September. It was his first game in more than a month.

Things didn't go well. Brisbane lost the match 16.16 (112) to 11.8 (74) and Neale injured his calf.

Season-ending was a common assessment of the extent of the damage. He'd likely need four to six weeks for recovery.

Eric Hipwood was already out for the rest of the year. He missed the Geelong game with a partial tear in his left ACL. He was to have surgery in the hope that he would be back on the field again in 2026.

Losing Neale for the rest of the finals would be a major blow to the Lions' hopes. Fagan seemed almost resigned to that outcome.

"Looks like he's done a calf, so that's not a good thing," Fagan had said after the Lions returned to Brisbane.

Was he worried that not having Neale would impact severely on premiership hopes?

"He's a great player so obviously he helps, and we've got quite a few other guys who are injured at the moment and not playing, so whether that adds up to too many injuries ... makes it difficult," Fagan said.

The loss to Geelong raised further questions. How would the Lions recover with a rematch in the Grand Final a possibility?

There won't be an overreaction, Fagan said.

We'll just do what we always do, have a look at the vision and find out where we made errors, and how we can improve.

For next week, it'll just be as simple as that.

I've got a lot of faith in this group.

We can make a drama out of it, but they've been in the last seven final series and done some pretty good work in that time.

It's not always going to be a bed of roses.

Every now and then you're going to meet an opponent, like we did, who were red-hot.

We'll just stay calm and do what we always do.

Neale initially was told he had only a 5% chance of playing again in 2025.

That was enough to motivate him to "have a crack."

How tough is Lachie Neale? So tough!

Hope of a comeback hinged on an extreme rehabilitation regime. He spent more than 60 hours in a hyperbaric chamber to accelerate tissue healing and reduce inflammation. High-performance manager Josh Low devised a five-day-on, two-day-off chamber protocol over three weeks, supplemented with therapy and targeted physiotherapy sessions.

Neale sharpened his mental focus, deleting all social media apps and devoting himself fully to recovery.

No one was certain he would make it, but as the Grand Final drew close and the Lions seemed set to be in it, speculation mounted about a possible return on Saturday 27 September, the decider.

The club announced its final team list on Thursday, 25 September. Neale was in it!

He had completed unrestricted sessions on the Tuesday and Thursday and met all medical and performance criteria.

In the Thursday training run at Ikon Park, Neale completed a full-intensity session, hitting top speed without pain, convincing the medical staff and coach Fagan that he could be cleared. Dayne Zorko later recalled that Neale sprinted 30 metres at "afterburner" pace during that session, showing he had full strength and confidence in his leg.

He was good to go.

There was a further surprise, however. He wasn't in the run-on list on Grand Final day. He was on the bench as the tactical sub and did not appear in the first half.

Fagan had known he'd probably need to call on Neale at some point, particularly if the scores were close and the game was in the balance.

It was tight at half time, the scores locked. Fagan believed Neale's fresh legs and clearance power could swing momentum.

Neale was "activated" as the team's sub at half-time. He was sent on for teenager Sam Marshall.

Neale's second-half impact was striking; he collected 17 disposals, seven clearances, and kicked an important third-quarter goal.

Was Fagan always confident in the impact Neale would have?

"I felt that if he (Neale) started and ran out of gas, that might be a bit of a spirit killer for the boys," Fagan said afterwards.

"But... if he could come on around about halftime and do what he did, it would be an enormous spirit lifter for us."

Brisbane scored back-to-back goals in quick succession through the brilliance of Charlie Cameron and established a 13-point lead late in the third term.

After what happened in the Qualifying Final, no one was prepared to rule the Cats out, especially in such a low-scoring game.

Enter Lachie Neale.

This is what the third quarter looked like after Neale's entry into the game:

- Brisbane straight away ramped up the pressure and won four free kicks in the first six minutes.
- Neale was involved in several early possessions. He had an important clearance and set up forward entries.
- Charlie Cameron kicked pivotal back-to-back goals, supported by Neale's handballs and ball movement.
- Neale had his own moment of brilliance with a long-range running goal at the 20-minute mark, just short of three-quarter time. Brisbane clearly had momentum.
- Brisbane finished the quarter with a significant lead, dominating clearances and creating decisive inside-50s. Geelong was wilting.

At three-quarter time, the Lions led 11.8 (74) to the Cats' 6.5 (41), a 33-point margin.

Neale wasn't done.

He added six clearances (seven for the half), the best of all players, and helped Brisbane dominate from centre bounces and stoppages.

The Lions put the Cats away in the fourth quarter for a 47-points victory, 18.14 (122) to 11.9 (75).

How did Neale feel as he prepared to take his place?

He conceded he had been the "most nervous" he'd ever been during a game as he ran to his position.

"I felt like a supporter, riding all the waves – I was probably the most nervous I've ever been in a game of football with the scores tied in a Grand Final... tight in a grand final and limited prep. Yeah, it's a little bit easier when everyone is tired and you're fresh. I felt like I covered the ground pretty well," he said.

His role as co-captain had been curtailed somewhat and after the final siren he remained modest about his contribution.

"I haven't done a whole lot of captaining the last few weeks – it's been Harris (Andrews)," he said. *"I can't take too much credit, and guys like 'Hughy' and 'Dunks' have steered the ship the last six or seven weeks while I've been missing in action.*

"So proud of this group, bloody hell. Pretty speechless. That performance was hard to describe. When we're on, we're on."

Josh Dunkley, said to have been convinced to join the Lions in 2023 during a meal with Neale and Andrews, was a key player for the Lions and his premiership experience with the Bulldogs (at 19 the youngest player in the team's 2016 victory) was an asset.

Having had his colours lowered a few weeks previously by Gold Coast's Josh Rowell (eventual Brownlow Medal winner), Dunkley hit back in the Grand Final.

Dunkley was modest about his own contribution, preferring to laud the efforts of key teammates.

"I thought Charlie was unbelievable... and the role that Lachie played, it was another selfless act from him," Dunkley said.

"He just said, 'I want to be involved and I don't really care

where I'm playing or if I'm the sub, that's all good.' So to have that presence of mind to be able to do that and come on and then dominate in the second half, he's such a special player. It is just a great team. And Harris Andrews, what else can you say? He is just an unbelievable player."

But Dunkley's own contribution was something special – he put on 18 tackles, the first player to do so in an AFL finals match.

Neale wasn't the only one who had felt a touch of nerves. Chris Fagan described having a "nervous night's sleep" over the decision to name him in the side.

"I was lying in bed last night thinking I was going to either look like a total idiot or a total genius after today's game. If we had lost, and he had only played a half, we would probably be bemoaning the fact we went about it in that way," he said.

"But the bottom line was this: Lachie was fit to play, but how much game time could he play?

"Basically, he had played one game in eight weeks, one game in 56 days. Coming into a Grand Final, I was a little bit worried about his ability to see the whole game out if he actually started."

It was Neale's presence in the mid-field for the second half that helped turn the game around for the Lions. It was a brave call by Fagan to use him as a "pinch-hitter."

Genius had prevailed, on two counts.

Brisbane club president Andrew Wellington was in no doubt about Fagan's ability.

"He's absolutely a favourite son and I think he deserves now to be spoken about as one of the really great coaches," Wellington told *foxsports.com.au*.

"I'll leave it to others to say whether he is one of the greats, but I think to win two flags back-to-back and play in three grand finals, play in seven final series, that's a huge effort. And we faced a lot of challenges this year.

"Last year, the challenges of the first half of the year were well documented, but we actually ended up with a pretty stable group for the back half of the year. This year, right through the season, we had players coming in and out with injury. We had a tough draw and... obviously we had a disappointing qualifying final against Geelong, so we had to go the long way round.

"I can understand why most people thought Geelong would have the wood on us, having watched the qualifying final, but it was a great effort by Chris to get the match-ups right and get the players up for it.

"And I think I heard someone say that they thought picking Lachie Neale was one of the riskiest decisions they'd seen that there ever was and there were doctors who are outside the club saying that we were crazy.

"But it was an inspired decision and having him as sub and having him come on the second half and play as effectively as he did was great."

In the aftermath, many of the AFL clubs expressed displeasure with the tactical-substitute system. Late in 2025 new AFL football boss Greg Swann (formerly with Brisbane) announced it was being scrapped for the 2026 season onwards.

Clubs instead would name 23 players for their match-day teams, including five on the interchange bench. The number of rotations would stay at 75 per match.

The "medical substitute" system was introduced for the 2021 season after the AFL doubled to 12 days the mandatory time out of the game for a player who suffered a concussion.

It was replaced by a "tactical substitute" system in 2023 allowing clubs to replace a player with an unused substitute at any stage of the game, for any reason. The two-year-old "medical reason" rule for a substitution no longer applied. A substituted player could not rejoin the game.

The change for the 2026 season meant there was no limit on the number of times a player can be interchanged (substituted) during a game.

LACHIE NEALE

Lachlan Oliver Neale was born on 24 May 1993 in Naracoorte, South Australia, and lived for a short time in Langkoop, Victoria, before moving to Kybybolite, South Australia.

He started playing football for Kybybolite in 2004 as a 10-year-old. He kicked eight goals for the year as his team won the under-14 KNTFL premiership alongside future AFL player Jack Trengove (Melbourne and Port Adelaide).

Neale played all his junior football for Kybybolite, then the Glenelg Football Club in the South Australian National Football League (SANFL). He was drafted to Fremantle with their fourth selection (number 58 overall) in the 2011 AFL draft, and made his AFL debut in Round 4, 2012, against St Kilda. Neale played for the Fremantle Dockers from 2012 to 2018 - 35 games and 67 goals. He won Doig Medals (best and fairest) in 2026 and 2018.

He was traded to the Brisbane Lions in 2019. He was premiership captain in 2024 and won the Brownlow Medal in 2020 and 2023.

2025: GETTING IT DONE

"We have become a really good finals team."

Chris Fagan's understatement after the 2025 Grand Final

Locked at 36-points apiece at half time and facing a lopsided early free-kick count that favoured Geelong (17-4), the defending premiers desperately needed a second-half surge.

A flurry of goals in the last-quarter turned a possible close game into an emphatic 47-point victory (122 to 75) in front of 100,022 spectators at the MCG on the last Saturday in September 2025.

Coached astutely by Chris Fagan, the Lions sealed back-to-back premierships, something they'd not achieved for two decades. The Brisbane Lions were underdogs, despite being reigning premiers.

They had beaten Geelong twice in the home-and-away season, 70-61 in Round 3 and 92-52 in Round 15. But it was the big loss in the qualifying final on 5 September, 112-74, that caused a rethink among the pundits.

To the betting agencies (football betting is legal much to the chagrin of many people) Geelong was the team to beat. Some were offering as much as $2.65 about Brisbane head-to-head.

Geelong was favoured by most commentators to win by a margin of up to 20 points.

But the Lions were not without support from media pundits. Abbey Holmes (Channel 7) predicted Brisbane to win by 2 points, nominating Will Ashcroft as her choice for the Norm Smith Medal.

She was among those who thought Brisbane could pull it off, citing the team's midfield depth and the return of key players such as Lachie Neale (she didn't know what role he would play at the time) and Jarrod Berry who would enable the contested possessions to fall Brisbane's way. Correct.

She might have been out by a good way in the margin, despite looking to be near the mark at half-time, but how right she was about the Lions' midfield!

The Lions won the contested possessions 149-141, possibly a closer result than some thought, but they dominated after half-time when it mattered most.

Will Ashcroft (Norm Smith Medal), Jaspa Fletcher and Hugh McCluggage provided the mid-field spark that saw the Lions home; a pair of 21-year-olds with McCluggage the older/wiser head at 27. Outside the midfield specialists, Zac Bailey, Harris Andrews (co-captain) and Dayne Zorko (former captain) were among Brisbane's best. Zorko was the elder statesman at 36 years old and in his 15th season.

In contrast to their Qualifying Final win, Geelong players could not assert themselves at stoppages. Brisbane reversed the clearance differential and controlled the contested game in the second half.

And there was THAT master stroke.

It was a bold decision to name Lachie Neale as the tactical substitute, considering his limited preparation after a calf injury. Fagan held Neale back to unleash him to break open what looked like being close after a deadlocked first half.

Neale's introduction swung the momentum Brisbane's way; he finished with 17 disposals, seven clearances, and a crucial goal.

The tactical move was a turning point.

Brisbane ended up dominating most statistics: Disposals 361-319; Inside 50s 66-51 (21-7 in the final term); clearances 7-52; marks 93-70; kicks 230-199; possession (%) 41-22; tackles 76-51.

The only stats where Geelong won were hit-outs, 141-64, suggesting they didn't make adequate use of the ball they won. Geelong had more turnovers, 61-57.

It didn't help Geelong that two of their star players collided in the second term, Jeremy Cameron suffering a broken arm which saw him subbed out in the third quarter, and Patrick Dangerfield who was well down on form, managing only 10 disposals for the game before being forced off.

Some commentators tipped Brisbane because they had been "as confident as any team in the competition interstate" and had demonstrated the ability to respond to adversity better than most.

Chris Fagan tweaked the Lions tactics from the Qualifying Final loss; key areas including clearances, midfield dominance and ball movement all improved.

The introduction into the game of Neale was pivotal, but Brisbane's key players, including Charlie Cameron who kicked four goals and Will Ashcroft who had 32 possessions, started the Lions' charge. The efficiency of Hugh McCluggage was also a factor as the Lions absorbed the early pressure, then punished the Cats in counter-attack. Dunkley's tackling was invaluable.

The Lions' defensive setup neutralised the expected dominance of Patrick Dangerfield in particular, Brandon Starcevich shutting him down in the first three quarters before 'Danger' was forced off after a head knock. His 10 disposals, without any clearances or goals, was a pale version of his preliminary final performance where he had 31 disposals and kicked three goals.

Dangerfield and Cameron, two of Geelong's most important players, were sorely missed after half-time.

The Cats had territorial advantages early after half-time and kicked four late (consolation) goals, but Brisbane's pressure and quicker transitions in the final quarter sealed the game.

Brisbane outplayed Geelong in a clinical second half, dominating contested play and inside-50 entries late in the game.

As Brisbane surged, Geelong was at a loss as how to stop the onslaught, conceding 13 goals to six after halftime, with many of Geelong's goals coming in "junk time" when the result was already decided.

The Cats failed to capitalise on their early dominance, despite a heavily favourable free-kick count. They missed several shots and did not convert their territorial advantage into scoreboard pressure.

Defensive errors allowed Brisbane to punish the Cats repeatedly on turnovers and rebounds.

Chris Scott had been aiming at his third flag in 15 seasons, but the players' third-term surrender denied him the chance.

"It's, obviously, difficult for us right at the moment, but I think in the fullness of time, when you sit back and think about the quality of team that beat us in this Grand Final, it will ease the pain a little bit," Scott said.

Chris Fagan after the game: "I have got a saying that's up on our wall – it's a famous Nelson Mandela quote. 'We never win. We never lose. We either win or we learn', and that's the attitude we have tried to take.

"I think everybody has embraced that at the footy club. We don't get too upset when we lose. Today is probably a good example. We got a lesson from Geelong three weeks ago (and) we went to work on it. We, obviously, had to win three finals to get another chance. Hopefully, today you saw we learnt some things from that game and did some things better.

"I always talked about failing our way to the top, and that's what we did. We got into some finals and for the first three years, I think we won one out of six finals and had a few lessons. Since that point in time, we have become a really good finals team.

"We did it the hard way again, to play four finals, I think that suits us."

How the match unfolded:

First Quarter

The opening quarter was a tense, low-scoring affair dominated by stoppages and defensive pressure. Kai Lohmann scored Brisbane's only goal late in the quarter. The Cats had two by the break and led by just three points after Zac Bailey had "radar" trouble with four behinds in the Lions' score.

Quarter time: Geelong 2.3 (15) – Brisbane 1.6 (12).

Second Quarter

Geelong extended the lead early in the second quarter, but the Lions responded with three consecutive goals as they reclaimed the momentum. By half-time, though, the scores were level. So were the key statistics and the match for all intents and purposes was in the balance. Yet, there were signs the Lions were settling into their trademark marking and ball-movement style. The Cats were doing well in the free-kick count to get a good share of possession.

Half-time: Geelong 5.6 (36) – Brisbane 5.6 (36)

Third Quarter

Often said to be the premiership quarter, the third quarter looked likely to be so.

Brisbane slowly but surely took control after an early score by Geelong.

A long bomb by Neale seemed to light a fuse.

The Lions midfield players came into their own and set up three quick goals late in the quarter for a 19-point lead at the final break.

Geelong started to look as though they were out of their depth as the Lions' tide surged.

Three-quarter time: Brisbane 9.9 (63) – Geelong 6.8 (44).

Final Quarter

The Lions started the final term as they finished the third and quickly added to their lead. Charlie Cameron's fourth goal and a burst of scoring from Rayner, Ashcroft and McCluggage extended the lead beyond the Cat's reach. Brisbane put on nine goals in the final term.

Geelong added some respectability late but Brisbane's dominance in contested possession and inside-50s through the second half enabled them to overwhelm the Cats.

Geelong went into the Grand Final having not lost a game in the play-offs to that point.

They'd beaten the Lions 16.16 (112) to 11.8 (74) in the qualifying final just three weeks previously, the Lions' only loss in the finals series.

Lachie Neale's remarkable 22-day recovery from a torn calf to a Grand Final culminated in a second successive premiership, a game-defining goal, and a second-half performance of which there had been few better.

The Lions kicked 13 to six goals after the main break.

Final score: BRISBANE 18.14 (122) – GEELONG 11.9 (75).

Brisbane goals: Cameron 4, McCluggage 4, Bailey 3, Lohmann 2, L. Ashcroft, W. Ashcroft, Morris, L. Neale, Rayner.
Geelong goals: Dempsey 4, Blicavs, Bowes, Close, Holmes, Mannagh, Mullin, S. Neale.
Best, Brisbane: W. Ashcroft, McCluggage, Andrews, Bailey, C. Cameron, Gardiner. Geelong: Dempsey, Holmes, Humphries, Atkins, Smith.
Injuries: Starcevich (Brisbane), J. Cameron (Geelong).
Norm Smith Medal: W. Ashcroft.

The teams:
Brisbane
FB: D.Zorko, D.Gardiner, R.Lester

HB: D.Wilmot, H.Andrews, B.Starcevich
C: H.McCluggage, L.Neale, L.Ashcroft
HF: C.Cameron, T.Gallop, Z.Bailey
FF: C.Rayner, L.Morris, C.Ah Chee
FO: D.Fort, J.Dunkley, W.Ashcroft
IC: K.Lohmann, J.Fletcher, S.Marshall, B.Reville, O.McInerney
EMG: S.Day, J.Tunstill, D.Joyce

Geelong
FB: C.O'Sullivan, S.De Koning, J.Henry
HB: M.O'Connor, Z.Guthrie, L.Humphries
C: G.Miers, M.Holmes, O.Dempsey
HF: B.Close, S.Mannagh, T.Stengle
FF: S.Neale, J.Cameron, P.Dangerfield
FO: R.Stanley, B.Smith, T.Atkins
IC: J.Bowes, O.Mullin, M.Blicavs, J.Martin, J.Clark
EMG: M.Knevitt, J.Bews, O.Henry

Brisbane's run to the Grand Final: defeated Fremantle 101-44, defeated Hawthorn 89-79, lost to Geelong 74-112, defeated Gold Coast 100-47, defeated Collingwood 100-71.

BRISBANE CLUB AWARDS 2025
Rookie of the Year: Levi Ashcroft
Marcus Ashcroft Most Professional Player Award: Hugh McCluggage
Shaun Hart Trademark Player of the Year: Josh Dunkley
Players' Player of the Year: Josh Dunkley
Finals Player Award: Harris Andrews

Youi Game Changer Award: Zac Bailey
Life Memberships: Greg Swann and Eric Hipwood

Time to Part-ee

The Brisbane Lions' 2025 premiership celebrations raged in the MCG rooms after the presentation of medals, continued at big gatherings in Fitzroy (spiritual home of the Lions) and in Brisbane.

The 2025 AFL Grand Final day coverage was the most-watched television program of the year, with a total audience of 6.1 million viewers across broadcast and streaming platforms.

The match itself drew 4.08 million viewers, with additional viewers tuning in for pre-match entertainment (thanks to the appearance by Snoop Dog no doubt) and post-match celebrations.

As Brisbane made sure of victory in the final term, Lions fans were in full voice, singing along with "Take Me Home, Country Roads" after Charlie Cameron's goals and roaring with every major score that made victory more emphatic.

Celebrations spilled on to the empty MCG after the presentation of medals. Players did a slow lap with the cup, soaking up the moment with the Brisbane fans who had stayed in the stands.

(Airlines and airports reported "thousands" of Brisbane Lions supporters flew from Brisbane to Melbourne with extra flights and several thousand extra seats scheduled. Melbourne Airport reported about 120,000 total arrivals across all passengers over the Grand Final period, noting that travelling Lions supporters were a noticeable component of the influx.)

The party in the MCG rooms was nothing short of raucous. The club song "The Pride of Brisbane Town" sung to the tune of the French national anthem, "La Marseillaise," was belted out by all.

Players doused each other – and Chris Fagan – with sports drink and there was plenty of joking around.

There may have been one or two beers consumed. In short, it was a celebration befitting the back-to-back premiership.

At night, the party moved to a South Yarra venue, many players showing their skill – even lack of it – on the dance floor.

Next morning almost all the players were a bit "dusty" but still full of "bonhomie" and fit enough to head off to the Brunswick Street Oval in Fitzroy for a fan day at the club's original homeland.

In Brisbane on game day, big crowds gathered at various venues, including The Pineapple Hotel (a popular venue for fans on game day when the Lions are playing interstate) and at and under landmarks, such as the Story Bridge, to watch and then celebrate the win.

The club and Brisbane City organised a "Back-to-Back Celebration" event in Queens Gardens in the CBD on Tuesday 30 September. The fans turned up in droves to celebrate the Lions squad and the Cup.

There was a fallout from the MCG celebrations for one prominent Lions fan. Photos emerged months later of Sports and Communications Minister Anika Wells on the ground with her husband. Controversy ensued over the minister's travel expenditure and whether the Grand Final trip (and others) complied with parliamentary disclosure rules.

Unfurling of the flag and the opening round.

Meanwhile, the Lions set about their attempt at a three-peat in 2026 with a road trip around Queensland to show the 2024 and 2025 premiership cups. The road show took on regional Queensland and as far north as Thursday Island to allow fans a close-up look at the silverware.

The itinerary began at Hervey Bay before heading to Bundaberg, Rockhampton, Mackay and Airlie Beach, then Townsville. Then, it was across the Cape to Weipa, and on to Thursday and Horn Islands before returning to Cairns.

Next stop was the Sunshine Coast for the Lions 2026 Community Camp, before returning to Brisbane then heading west to Toowoomba and back for the Opening Round clash against the Western Bulldogs.

2024: THE DROUGHT BREAKS

"Victory is sweetest when you've known defeat."

Malcolm S. Forbes, publisher of *Forbes* magazine

Chris Fagan's Lions lost the 2023 decider by less than a goal. Such an outcome would have reduced many fans to tears, particularly as it was Collingwood that inflicted the defeat.

The match also was the Lions' fifth appearance in the finals since Fagan was appointed coach. Could a premiership be far away?

Chris Fagan was staring at a difficult season in 2024 after getting so close. It is always a challenge for a beaten Grand Final team to bounce back after a narrow loss in a game that could have been won.

Winning a premiership raises questions about a possible hangover the next season. A team that loses one by less than a goal (four points) can also suffer a hangover, or they can do what Chris Fagan's Lions did – hit back, convincingly.

It was a stern test of the mettle of Fagan and his players to "butter up" in 2024. But the coach had a mantra (his own, or perhaps one borrowed from a fictional character) to see him through.

"Be a goldfish. Move on."

Move, they did.

Brisbane defeated Sydney 18.12 (120) to 9.6 (60) at the MCG in front of more than 100,000 football fans, posting the largest margin in an AFL Grand Final since 2007.

The Lions dominated possession, taking 158 marks to Sydney's 88.

It was the Lions' first premiership since 2003. They led at every change, a run of six straight goals in the second quarter pretty much putting the game to bed.

A shaky start in 2024 suggested maybe the Lions did have a hangover.

At the halfway point of the season, few pundits gave Brisbane a chance – the team was outside the "four" after starting with three consecutive losses.

But they delivered one of the all-time great season recoveries, winning critical finals matches despite injuries and setbacks, and making history as the first premiership team coached by someone who never played an AFL game. That stat was largely irrelevant in the context of how Chris Fagan had resurrected the Lions.

Fagan knew he had a solid foundation to work with. The Lions fell only a week short of the decider in 2022 and 2020. They'd made the Grand Final in 2023 and as heart-breaking as the loss was, he would have believed success was coming.

Fagan also would have had other things on his mind through 2023 – the Hawthorn racism saga the principal one.

The players knew Fagan would have been struggling with the things going on outside his control as they headed into the season.

Then-captain Dane Zorko summed it up: "He's had a very difficult 13 months. He's put a lot aside and left a lot of things at the front door to come in and put on a brave face for us and coach us the way he has.

"He's been a phenomenal leader of this football club and continues to do so, and that's another thing that spurs us on to want to do well."

A year on and the Lions finished fifth on the ladder and were playing finals football again.

They had to win four games in four weeks after the home-and-away series ended. Also, they had to do something that the club had done only once in 38 years and 871 games – win three consecutive matches interstate.

They might have been travel-weary. The seasoned players among the pride would have to stand up and be counted.

Dayne Zorko and Lachie Neale had long been waiting for a premiership. It had been elusive – the 2024 decider was their 277th and 272nd game respectively.

Brisbane's 60-point win was better than the winning margins of the club's three previous flags – 26 points against Essendon in 2001, 9 points against Collingwood in 2002 and 50 points against Collingwood in 2003. The 2024 AFL Grand Final was the fourth decided by 60 points or more in the last six years.

For Will Ashcroft, winning the Norm Smith Medal consigned the disappointment of missing the 2023 Grand Final due to injury to the distant past. His 30 disposals and a goal were significant in the Lions' victory.

Logan Morris at 19 years of age was the youngest Brisbane player to play in a Grand Final (and the youngest player on the ground). He contributed two goals and was subbed off late in the game to ensure all in the squad could revel in the victory.

Other Lions who played their first games in 2024 were Bruce

Revell, Shadeau Brain, Brandon Ryan and Henry Smith.

There were seven Queenslanders in the 2024 premiership side – Harris Andrews, Will Ashcroft, Charlie Cameron, Jaspa Fletcher, Eric Hipwood, Jack Payne and Dayne Zorko.

The unfurling of the 2024 AFL premiership flag at the Gabba on Sunday 23 March 2025 brought together club legends Simon Black, Alastair Lynch, Chris Johnson, Jason Akermanis, and coach Leigh Matthews

They were celebrating something they last saw two decades before. The fans were there in force, 30,012 of them.

The unfurling ended a 21-year wait for fans, legends of the past and a new generation.

The significance of the Grand Final win was bigger than just one game. The 2024 flag represented Brisbane's rise from 13th on the ladder mid-season to nailing the premiership, only the second club this century to win it from outside the top-four at the halfway point.

In summary, Brisbane's 2024 premiership was characterised by overwhelming grand final dominance, a dramatic mid-season turnaround, strategic excellence, and deep emotional resonance for players, coaches, and fans alike.

Lifetime Lions fan **Sam Harvey**: Everywhere you looked, there was a story of redemption. I was so proud:

- Will Ashcroft, the second-youngest Norm Smith Medallist.
- Lachie Neale and Harris Andrews, Premiership captains.
- Cal Ah Chee, 4 goals after being subbed out in 2023.
- Kai Lohmann, 4 goals after battling injury after injury.
- Ryan Lester and Dayne Zorko, brothers-in-law who stayed loyal through our darkest days.

- Darcy Fort, who stepped up in Oscar's absence.
- Jack Payne, whose tackle in the saved our season.
- Joey kicking the last goal, a much-maligned career finishing with a premiership.

"Watching Fages breakdown when he hugged club legend Leigh Matthews choked everyone up. Lethal who was a board member and mentor to Fagan said to him before the game 'You're a premiership coach and they've got to prove whether they're a premiership team,' before embracing him after the game saying, 'I told you that you were a premiership coach and you've got a premiership team... can't be more pleased for you'.

Fagan stressed the Grand Final "wasn't about" him.

"I don't see it that way, but it is fantastic to be part of a journey to start working with a group of players that were a long way off being a winning team to now where this is our fifth year of being really competitive," he said.

"We've been close to getting to the big dance a few times but not close enough, so to get there is just a tremendous reward for everybody at the footy club, not just me, but the players, the staff and everybody who has done the hard yards because there have been a lot of hard yards done."

QUARTER-BY-QUARTER SCORES –

Quarter-time: BRISBANE 4.3 (27) – SYDNEY 3.1 (19).
Half-time: BRISBANE 11.7 (73) – SYDNEY 4.3 (27).
Three-Quarter time: BRISBANE 16.11 (107) – SYDNEY 5.4 (34).
FULL-TIME: BRISBANE 18.12 (120) – SYDNEY 9.6 (60).
Brisbane goals: Ah Chee and Lohman 4, Daniher and Morris 2, Ashcroft, Berry, Cameron, Hipwood, McCluggage, Rayner.

Brisbane's best: Will Ashcroft (Norm Smith Medallist), Neale, Ah Chee, Daniher, Lohmann, McCluggage.

Club awards 2024

Rookie of the Year: Logan Morris

Marcus Ashcroft Most Professional Player Award: vice-captain Hugh McCluggage.

Shaun Hart Trademark Player Award: Oscar McInerney

Players' Player of the Yea: Josh Dunkley

Best Finals Player: Four-way tie – Brandon Starcevich, Will Ashcroft, Lachie Neale, Callum Ah Chee

Youi Game Changer Award (weekly fan vote): Cam Rayner

AFL ALL-AUSTRALIAN TEAM 2024

Lachie Neale (interchange)

22 matches in 2024; 13 goals, 4 behinds.

Averages: 29.5 disposals, 75.7% disposal efficiency, 13.7 contested possessions, 7.5 clearances, 2.5 centre clearances, 3.2 tackles, 6.8 score involvements and 4.8 inside 50s.

Dayne Zorko (half-back)

23 matches in 2024; 7 goals, 6 behinds.

Averages: 26.0 disposals, 78.0% disposal efficiency, 8.2 marks, 1.1 intercept marks, 0.7 spoils and 4.1 rebound 50s.

The All Australian team is selected from a previously named All Australian Squad. Other Brisbane players named in the squad were Harris Andrews, Joe Daniher and Cameron Rayner.

A LONG WAY TO THE TOP

"Success consists of going from failure to failure without loss of enthusiasm."

Winston Churchill

As far as top-class AFL players wanting to join the Brisbane Lions was concerned, the club until 2017 seemed to be on the nose.

In fact, some players were even so disillusioned they made it known they were keen to leave. A group that wanted out in 2013 – Jared Polec, Patrick Karnezis, Billy Longer, Sam Docherty, and Elliot Yeo, were referred to as the "Go-home Five." All requested trades back to their respective home states.

How did they fare after leaving?

Elliot Yeo went to West Coast (All-Australian selection), Sam Docherty (Carlton, All-Australian), Jared Polec (Port Adelaide, good season in 2014 but not much after that), Billy Longer (St Kilda, retired early after concussions and other injuries), Patrick Karnezis (Collingwood, mostly in the VFL).

The Lions finished 12th in 2013, 15th in 2014 and 17th in 2015 and 2016.

At the end of the 2016 season, the Lions had won only three of their 22 home-and-away games, only just ahead of cellar-dwellers Essendon on percentage. The Lions managed to outscore four other teams over the season with 1,770 points (including Essendon by 333), but the other side of the ledger showed their defence was leaking serious "oil". They'd conceded the most points of all 18 teams, 2,872 – 516 more than last-placed Essendon.

How were the Lions going to stop the rot?

The first casualty was coach Justin Leppitsch. Chris Fagan arrived in time for the start of the 2017 season.

There was no immediate improvement through Fagan's first year – in fact the Lions were wooden-spooners. A priority was going to be some serious work on the defensive set-up.

One answer was to add some experienced players to the list, notably Luke Hodge from Hawthorn in 2018.

Lions defensive coach Murray Davis (later to join the Adelaide Crows) played a pivotal role. He emphasised the importance of experience to provide structure to the defensive unit.

The group's mindset changed. The defence regrouped, became "stingier" and prevented oppositions from getting on scoring runs. The backline tightened up one-on-one contests and focused on winning ground-balls.

The following seasons saw some more important additions to the defensive line-up

Harris Andrews, who was already at the club but developed into a premier key defender and co-captain, went on to earn All-Australian honours multiple times.

Jack Payne, drafted in 2017, established himself as a strong key defender.

Brandon Starcevich, drafted in 2017, also became an important defensive player, known for his intercept marking and disposal efficiency.

Marcus Adams was recruited in 2019, but injuries reduced his game time.

In seasons 2024-2025, the Lions' key defensive unit was led by Harris Andrews, Jack Payne, Tom Doedee and Ryan Lester.

Brandon Starcevich had been a crucial shutdown-player and he would be missed in 2026, but defensive options remained strong: Ryan Lester, Harris Andrews, Jack Payne, Tom Doedee, Darcy Wilmot, Conor McKenna and Darragh Joyce would all have a part to play. Emerging defenders such as James Tunstill and Luke Beecken would most likely get their chance, too.

The result of Fagan's new approach and the recruitment program was a sharp reduction in points conceded per game. The Lions became one of the AFL's most difficult sides to score against.

This was in stark contrast to the final years of Justin Leppitsch's term.

Leppitsch had been a favourite son in Brisbane, selected at pick four by the then Brisbane Bears in the 1992 AFL draft.

He made his debut in 1993 for the Bears as a 17-year-old, but injury put him out of the game for 15 months. When he returned from a knee reconstruction, he went on to become a key member of the Lions squad formed when Fitzroy and Brisbane merged in 1997.

In 1999 under new coach Leigh Matthews, he won Brisbane's Best and Fairest award, was selected as All Australian for the first time and represented Australia in International Rules.

He played at centre half-back in the club's three premiership sides from 2001 to 2003 under Matthews and earned All Australian status three times.

A chronic hamstring-related back injury forced him from the game in June 2006.

In October 2006, Leppitsch became an assistant coach to Leigh Matthews. Then, he joined Richmond as an assistant coach in September 2009, also the last year Matthews was in charge of the Lions. Michael Voss, another favourite son for 269 games with the Lions, became senior coach until he was told his contract would not be renewed in 2014.

To make things worse in 2013, the club's most decorated champion, Simon Black, announced his retirement.

The Lions board apparently decided to stick with someone they'd known as a player. Leppitsch was inducted into the Brisbane Lions Hall of Fame in 2012. In 2013, he was signed to three-year contract to be senior coach. Several players already were contemplating leaving the club by then.

As was the case for Michael Voss, things did not go well for Leppitsch. The Lions were going nowhere and Leppitsch became a casualty.

To make things worse in 2016, Daniel Merrett, Trent West, and Justin Clarke retired; Jackson Paine, Josh Watts, Josh McGuinness, Hugh Beasley, and Billy Evans were delisted; and Pearce Hanley was traded to Port Adelaide. Half a run-on side was gone.

The playing list needed an overhaul, but few experienced players would be willing to go to a club that, frankly, was at rock-bottom.

What would it take to make Brisbane a destination club? A coach with a new approach.

In previous years, Paul Roos, a former Lions player and successful coach with the Sydney Swans had been on Brisbane's shopping list. In August 2013, then Lions chairman Angus Johnson said Roos had confirmed he would not be going to Brisbane. Johnson said in a letter to members: "He contacted me... and informed me that, due to family reasons, he would be unable to relocate to Brisbane and was therefore ruled out as a candidate."

First Voss, then Leppitsch, had been brought in to turn things around. They couldn't get it done. What next?

There was trouble within club management.

After the sacking of Michael Voss as senior coach (fearing that certain players would refuse to play if Voss's contract was renewed) and Paul Roos saying "no" to the job, Leigh Matthews joined directors Paul Williams and Mick Power in a push to overthrow Angus Johnson and the majority of the board. There was internal turmoil over a botched move to relocate the club HQ to a new site. History shows that turmoil in football committees can mutate into trouble on the field.

In English football, Sir Alex Ferguson's retirement in 2013 at Manchester United triggered years of board indecision, poor managerial hires, and over one billion pounds in spending without a Premier League title. The lack of clear strategy led to repeated early European competition exits and inconsistent league finishes, dropping from champions to mid-table challengers.

Leadership changes, public board fights or uncertainty about key staff (CEO, football manager, senior coach) can create anxiety for players and coaches, who start worrying about job security and future direction instead of performance and improvement. This can result in lost trust in decision-making and distract from game preparation. Match-day performance can also be affected by such rumblings off the field. This seemed to be the case at MU. Was it happening at Brisbane?

In September 2013, Bob Sharpless was elected chairman, heading a new-look board that included Leigh Matthews, Mick Power, Cameron Milner and Peter McGregor.

Matthews, who coached the Lions' to three Premierships between 2001-2003, joined the Board as Football Director, previously having been "expertise Director."

With a new-look board and Leppitsch installed as new coach fans probably were right to feel a little more optimistic.

But all that came unstuck as the Lions slid down the AFL ladder over three successive years.

When Sharpless stood down as chairman at the club's AGM in 2017, the Lions didn't have much to show success-wise for their re-birth

The Year of the Lion was still nearly a decade away, but the seeds of something big were being sown.

Greg Swann had been appointed CEO of the Club, David Noble was appointed General Manager of Football and a new Senior Coach was being sought.

Sharpless said at the AGM as he stood down: "When I first became Chairman, the Club had a number of issues, where we had a lot of unhappiness within the football club.

"For me the last four years have been about trying to resolve those issues, appointing the right people for positions and campaigning for a new training and administration base, which the Club most desperately needs."

By the time of the 2017 AGM, the Lions had their new head coach: Chris Fagan.

The Lions interview panel saw Fagan as the ideal person to rekindle the enthusiasm of the Lions players and fans.

Sam Harvey:

A panel featuring Peter Schwab, Talent Acquisition and Retention Manager Matti Clements (a director and senior psychologist at Mental Edge Consulting) and Simon Black who was at the time an assistant coach at the Lions, shortlisted four names for the role: Brett Ratten, Brett Montgomery, John Barker and Chris Fagan, with press reports suggesting the choice came down to Fagan and Barker.

Swann and Schwab chatted to Fagan in his Box Hill (Melbourne) home and were really captivated by his passion, Schwab telling *Brisbane Lions Media*, "You are always looking for the best overall candidate, but we especially wanted someone who could establish strong personal relationships... unite the group for a common cause."

Fagan was a different type of candidate, 10 years older than the other prospects; he had a wealth of experience working with players, was a teacher by profession and had a keen eye in relationship-building and growth-mindset, two areas the Lions desperately craved.

Speaking to a live audience on the *Roar Deal Podcast*, featuring Michael Whiting and Dom Fay at the Brisbane Powerhouse, Fagan shared a unique insight into his first week as the new Brisbane Lions coach.

"When I first got the job, I thought I needed to get everyone on the same page with me. So, we organised a two-day seminar with all the other football department staff. I spoke to them about my philosophy on things, what I was going to try and do with the Brisbane Lions, and how I'd like them to be a part of that and help me," Fagan said.

Fagan's philosophical outlook was a breath of fresh air for a club needing something different. What he said was simple but resonated with many of the people at the seminar, as more than 90% of them stayed on to taste the success in 2024.

Fagan explained: "Sometimes in leadership, you just have to have your plan. Don't be so stubborn that you won't change it from time to time, but don't give up on your principles or philosophies. Stick with them, and in the end, you'll come through. I think if you jump around all the time, responding to results and the narrative, you lose your way pretty quickly. I wanted to stand for something."

Remaining steadfast in your beliefs can come at a cost, as Australian Ange Postecoglou found when he took up a managerial job in the English Premier League with Tottenham Hotspur then Nottingham Forest. But that's another story.

With Fagan secured as the new coach and Andrew Wellington appointed as deputy chairman in December 2016 to eventually take over from Sharpless, the Lions began looking to secure a multi-million-dollar training base. This facility was to support all future Lions players, including the newly created AFLW side, which was to be coached by 1990 Collingwood Premiership player Craig Starcevich (uncle of Lion Brandon).

Fagan arrived at Brisbane in late 2016. He wasn't going to turn things around on the ladder immediately. In fact, the Lions slipped to last in his first year. That may have caused a few tremors in club ranks, but within two seasons Fagan had the Lions playing finals football.

Through a combination of strong leadership, smart recruiting, and a cultural rebuild, Fagan guided the Lions from the league's lowest point to sustained finals appearances, beginning in 2019, followed by three Grand Final appearances from 2023 and ultimately, the back-to-back premierships of 2024 and 2025.

Players began to see the Lions as a place where they could develop, compete for premierships, and be part of a positive, united environment.

The evidence: in the 2025 AFL trade period, two free agent players who could have gone anywhere were happy to pen their names to the Lions squad for 2026.

IN FAGES WE TRUST

Undoubtedly – and obviously to everyone – the Lions' biggest recruitment coup over the past decade was that of Chris Fagan as head coach.

He was recruited in October 2016 by a selection process involving a five-person panel led by then club CEO Greg Swann.

The panel interviewed several candidates but found Fagan to be the standout. The panel cited his elite knowledge, experience, mentoring skills, and communication abilities as ideal for the club's new direction.

His ability to create a strong club environment also was a key factor.

Fagan had significant previous AFL experience at Hawthorn and Melbourne, albeit not as senior coach.

Fagan brought a completely new approach to the Lions.

The shift involved assessing positional targets based on players' ability to buy into the Lions' team-first mentality and rebuilding ethos.

Players with strong leadership and high character took precedence over positional stars with individual ambitions.

Fagan's tenure marked a major cultural change: recruitment was more strategic, positional needs were prioritized according to the team's overall structure, and every new addition was thoroughly assessed for attitude and fit.

This is how **Sam Harvey** saw the impact of the arrival of Fagan in Brisbane:

There's no sugarcoating this: by the end of 2016, the Brisbane Lions were nothing short of a shambles.

With a dismal average home crowd of just 17,074 and a gut-wrenching average losing margin of 51 points per game, the Lions barely scraped above Essendon, whose roster was a patchwork of VFL top-up players.

Over the course of the season, the Lions conceded a staggering 2,872 points – an average of 131 per game and 79 more goals than the next-worst club.

To make matters worse, their most seasoned player and stalwart defender, Daniel Merrett, hung up his boots at the end of the season after a humiliating 200th game, in which St Kilda's Nick Riewoldt carved him up with 21 marks and 9 goals as the Saints piled on 25 goals.

This was the 11th time a club had kicked 20 or more goals against Brisbane in 2016 and the third time in four weeks that a club had kicked 25.

The writing was on the wall for the Lions' much-maligned coach, Justin Leppitsch. But the misery didn't end there. In fact, it started before the season began, with the loss of Merrett's heir apparent in defence, Justin Clarke, who had finished 10th in the Lions' best and fairest the previous year.

On 18 January, Clarke collided with a teammate's knee, leaving him unconscious for 15 seconds. Though Clarke was released from the hospital, he struggled with severe memory loss for weeks and was ultimately forced to announce his early retirement, on 31 March 2016 – at just 22 years old. It was a crushing blow to a team already reeling from misfortune, and an even harder pill to swallow for coach Justin Leppitsch, whose grip on the role had been slowly slipping away before the season had even started.

The Lions' record in 2016 was the culmination of a downward spiral that began with events between August and October 2013 and the sacking of favourite son and later Carlton coach Michael Voss with a record of 8-11 after 20 rounds.

Leppitsch accepted a poisoned chalice fully aware there was no quick fix.

At the start of his coaching tenure in 2014, Leppitsch implored the club to be patient with his audacious five-year plan to develop an attacking team, which he predicted would be heavily scored against in the interim. But after a 14-52 record over three years, with an average of 73.62 for and 111.97 against, the Lions bosses shied under mounting supporter pressure and unceremoniously sacked him.

Later, history would show that Leppitsch became an integral part of Damien Hardwick's juggernaut at the Tigers and Craig McRae's Magpies, being involved in four premierships as an assistant coach.

The Lions yearned for stability, yet always found themselves as the mythical Sisyphus did, pushing a rock up a bloody big hill. Newly appointed CEO Greg Swann found himself at loggerheads with Cricket Australia and former Gabba curator Kevin Mitchell Jr time and time again as the Lions, who represented all of Brisbane in the AFL, were unable to train at The Gabba, sometimes even until the week before the season started.

Trying to stabilise a young list when they're training at a smorgasbord of different grounds during pre-season is extremely difficult. This was the result of harsh restrictions on the Lions by curator Mitchell Jr who reportedly disliked Australian Rules Football and, anyway, wanted to prepare The Gabba for the summer of cricket.

There was possible good news in March 2025, when the Queensland Government announced that a 63,000-seat stadium to be built at inner-city Victoria Park (1km from the CBD) in time for the 2032 Olympic Games would become the Lions' new home (shared with cricket) from 2033. The Gabba (capacity 36,000) was going to be demolished.

The nomadic battle-scarred club moved between Giffin Park in Coorparoo, Leyshon Park in Yeronga, the University of Queensland Campus, Moreton Bay Central Sports Complex in Burpengary, South Pine Sports Complex in Brendale, Hickey Park in North Brisbane and Maroochydore Multi Sports Complex on the Sunshine Coast.

This malaise was reminiscent of the fate that befell the subjugated Fitzroy Football Club in their dying days; something needed to change to stop history repeating itself.

Swann got the call from the AFL that his expertise was needed in Brisbane and that call was then followed by one from Club Director Leigh Matthews and Chairman Bob Sharpless.

Swann joined during July 2014, signing on for four years which became a decade until his move to AFL headquarters in 2025.

The priority for Swann and Sharpless: Retain players and find a new training base.

The highly-rated David Noble was lured away from Adelaide to be the Lions football operations manager.

With Fagan secured as the new coach and Andrew Wellington appointed as deputy chairman in December 2016 to eventually take over from Sharpless, the Lions began looking to secure a multi-million-dollar training base. This facility was to support all future Lions players, including the newly created AFLW side.

Springfield had been touted as early as May 2013, when the Kevin Rudd Labor Government announced a $15 million Federal Government budget allocation. Only 23 days later, the newly elected Prime Minister Tony Abbott's Coalition Government rejected the budget, and the move to Springfield was abandoned.

Forward to the summer of 2017, and Lions General Manager – Infrastructure, Strategy, and Government Relations, Jake Anson, announced a new and revised plan to upgrade the block of land in Springfield and finally give the Lions a home.

Funding for the Springfield Project was pushed by the AFL after the Lions' AFLW team was unable to play their 2017 Grand Final at the Gabba. This was due to curator Mitchell Jr being unhappy with the damage caused by the Adele concert and wanting to fix the grass in time for the 2017-18 Ashes series between Australia and England.

The Gabba facilities were in a dire state, with Fagan even describing them as a dungeon: *It's pretty smelly in the dungeon of the Gabba. Seriously, they'd flush the sewage system, and it would stink the whole football department out. There were days when I told staff to go home; it made your eyes water, it was that bad. In its time, it was a great facility, but by the time I got there, it had been surpassed by most clubs that had grand facilities and multi-million-dollar setups. We only had that during footy season, because in the summer, we had to train at various venues around Brisbane where we could find some good grass. It was vastly different from what I was used to at the Hawthorn Football Club. That was one thing I wasn't accustomed to, and even if we did get to train at the Gabba, if we had two hours booked, that's all we got. The gate wouldn't open until 9:00, and it closed straight away at 11:00. We didn't even have the chance to do goal-kicking practice after training.*

The Lions were in such a precarious position that Fagan admitted if he had done more homework on the club, he may not have made the move to Brisbane: *I don't think I really did enough homework on the club, and if I did, I probably would have stayed at Hawthorn. I was that keen to coach, and I just figured a bloke like me – who didn't play AFL footy – was offered a coaching job, so I thought I just had to take what I could get and do the best that I could. It was a little bit of a private lifelong dream of mine to be an AFL coach, and it took me 55 years to get there, but I did. So, I came to the club and thought, 'I better learn a bit about it,' and there's nothing like talking to the people who are actually working here.*

It took Fagan three weeks to interview everyone at the club. He didn't have a time limit; if someone wanted to chat for 10 minutes, they were welcome to do so, and if they wanted to chat for two hours, Fagan was happy to soak up all the information like a sponge. Trying to keep it short and simple, Fagan asked everyone three questions:

1. What's good about this club?
2. What's not good about this club?

3. If you were me, what would you do to make this place successful and better?

Fagan credits the honesty from the staff and players. Yet, there was one comment that really stood out to him, explaining: *The biggest comment was that a lot of players at the time preferred to be injured and in rehab rather than play, which I was astonished by. But that was the honest truth. If you're saying that, you don't feel safe. If you don't have to play, you don't have to perform, and then you don't have to get feedback. I would say that maybe the environment was a fairly critical, in-your-face sort of place where the blame game might have been played a little too often. I'm only theorising about that – I wasn't there.*

I saw in that the opportunity. It took me a while to get the confidence of everybody that I wasn't going to react every time we lost a game of football, because I knew that where the club was at the time, it was going to take a bit of effort to climb up the ladder again. We were in a very bad place.

Fagan further explained that to turn Brisbane into a destination club, something had to change.

I don't mean this disrespectfully to the guys who were there at the time, but Brisbane had become a club that was attracting players from other clubs who couldn't get a game at those clubs. They were being really well paid by Brisbane, and they were just average footballers. Again, I'm not critical of them, but we needed to be better than that, he said.

The Lions decided to focus on good young country footballers, believing that country footballers often possessed unique qualities such as resilience, strong work ethic, and adaptability, traits highly valued in AFL environments.

With Pick 3 in the 2016 draft, the Lions selected goal-kicking midfielder "Rolls Royce" Hugh McCluggage from South Warrnambool, along with his best mate and Vic Country captain Jarrod Berry from Horsham, and half-back flanker Cedric Cox from Camperdown. The three had played together with the North Ballarat Rebels. The Lions also picked up Alex Witherden from Geelong Falcons and decided to take a punt on a 22-year-old, 206 cm gangly ruckman from the Casey Demons by the name of Oscar McInerney.

Fagan: *Fortunately, we were able to recruit some good young guys and invested games into them early. They weren't very good. We're talking about guys like McCluggage and Berry. It's amazing how, when they're not very good to start with, they can become so good. So, I just had to invest in those guys. It was about playing the long game. A lot of those guys were big in our finals campaign (2019) and in other campaigns as well. I just had to get the boys to understand what a growth mindset is.*

McCluggage and Berry have spoken extensively about Fagan's growth-mindset mantra, McCluggage telling Michael Whiting on *AFL.com.au* before the 2023 AFL Grand Final: "You hear a few things about what the club was like before you get here, and you watch a bit of media, and you see they're not going so well on the field first and off the field in a few different areas.

"Straight away, there was a massive change, and it goes to show that no matter where you're at, you can change things really quickly.

"We had a lot of good people here. We probably just didn't have the things in place to make sure we could get to a higher level as a club and team.

"Ever since then, I've been involved in a club that's hard-working and has a growth mindset. Everyone wants to improve all the time."

This growth mindset was evident straight away in Fagan's first couple of weeks at the helm, and he thanks his daughter Jessica for that: *I hadn't been a teacher for a long time in the true sense, although I think coaches are teachers. But I rang my daughter (Jessica), who is a secondary school teacher (she reluctantly followed her mum and dad into that profession), and I said, 'Oh Jess, what's the latest stuff going on in education?' She said, 'Growth mindset, Dad. A lady by the name of Carol Dweck wrote a book called* Growth Mindset.*'*

Fundamentally, that book is about making mistakes being okay – that's how you learn, that's how you get better. And how you treat those mistakes and failures is really important. I taught the boys about that and had to follow through with my words. We played games early days, and we lost. There wasn't a witch-hunt about who made what mistakes and whose fault it was that we lost. It was like, 'Okay, what happened today? What could we take from that, that will make us better in the future?' They probably got sick of me doing it, but I thought that was the only way back with them, because so many guys were lacking in confidence, and I knew the young guys starting were finding it tough. It was my job to keep the energy in the place, and then those boys started to emerge.

Although the Lions were defeated by eventual premiers Richmond in front of a packed Gabba and lost by a kick to the Giants in the Semi-Final, Fagan and the Football Department in 2019 had turned Brisbane into a destination club again.

THE PRIDE BEHIND THE SCENES

A strong supporting cast stands behind the success of Chris Fagan and his Brisbane Lions.

From family to confidants and club officials, team Fagan is a comprehensive assembly of supporters and specialists.

His family has stood behind him all the way through a career that has taken him from The Gravel at Queenstown in Tasmania to the hallowed turf of the MCG where he already has two premiership titles on his curriculum vitae.

The name Fagan is synonymous with Tasmanian football.

It was Chris's father who probably whetted his young son's appetite for coaching as he sat in the sheds watching his dad Austin Fagan inspire Queenstown players (he coached Smelters, Lyell and Gormanston) to be their best as they took on teams from around Tasmania's West Coast.

Austin Fagan was an electrician who worked in the mines in Queenstown. He instilled into his boys a passion for hard work and football.

Austin was a player of some note as a captain and coach with football clubs on the west coast of Tasmania. Chris's uncle Gerald also played for Smelters Robins in the WTFAL.

In the forward to a book about football in Queenstown, Chris Fagan wrote: "My Dad, Austin passed away on December 12th, 2019. He was a football legend on the West Coast, both as a player and coach. When I was a young bloke, he also wrote a column on West Coast Football for the *Advocate* newspaper. I can still remember reading his hand-written drafts every week before he handed them in for publishing. It was something I looked forward to with great anticipation and as it turns out was an important part of my football education. He wrote with passion and intelligence about the game and people he cherished. He coached with the similar empathy and care for his players. He passed on to me a love of the game and a great interest in coaching. He was a role model to me in the way he lived his life, his competitive instinct, his generosity towards people and the way he cared for our family."

The family remains close despite the distance that separates most of them these days.

A brother, Grant, has been a successful coach in his own right. He is regarded as the most successful Tasmanian coach from the last 20 years, including five statewide premierships with the Clarence Roos. He was a player at North Hobart and Sandy Bay before coaching at country level with Kingston.

Grant Fagan's coaching career to 2025:

- Coached Kingston to a Huon Football Association Premiership in 1991
- Assistant coach Clarence Football Club (TFL) 1993-1995 (2 Premierships and a Runner-Up)
- Coached Clarence Football Club (TFL) 1996-1998 and 2000 (3 Premierships and a Runner-Up)
- Created a family double in 2025 with brother Chris when the Roos won the Southern Football League Grand Final.

Grant also assisted with some of the football development

academy programs in Tasmania.

He was "Coach Inductee" No.230 in the Tasmanian Football Hall of Fame. Chris Fagan entered the Tasmanian Football Hall of Fame in 2007. His citation read: "Name almost any role within the sphere of football, and Chris Fagan has most likely mastered it. From the infamous 'Gravel' to the hallowed turf of the MCG and beyond, Fagan has carved out a career both on and off the field that very few can match for longevity or sustained excellence."

Two women have played an important part in Chris Fagan's life: his mother Beth and wife Ursula.

Beth Fagan says her husband Austin was a natural coach. She told ABC Hobart Breakfast presenter Tracey Strong that Austin was a natural footballer and cricketer who took on coaching after they got married.

The couple raised their four children on Tasmania's West Coast, before moving to Hobart when Chris, the eldest, was 15. His siblings are Grant, Anne-Marie and David.

"He was just a natural," she said of Austin. "He taught them everything about sport and how to conduct themselves and how to be good people. That's how we brought our kids up, never to look down on people."

Austin Fagan died in 2019. This was the family death notice:

FAGAN, Austin Michael

9.7.1934 - 12.12.2019 Passed away peacefully in his 86th year. Very much loved and loving husband of Beth of 59 years. Proud and cherished father and father-in-law of Chris and Ursula, Grant and Kym, Anne-Maree, David and Mandy. Adored Pa of his 11 grandchildren and great grandchildren.

Rest in peace Pa. Forever in our hearts.

Beth Fagan, now in her 80s, had much to celebrate towards the end of September 2025. First, she saw Grant coach Clarence to a premiership at home in Tasmania, then it was off to Melbourne a week later to see Chris collect back-to-back premiership trophies with the Brisbane Lions.

She said it was "amazing" watching Grant coach underdogs Clarence to victory over Lauderdale at North Hobart Oval.

"I'm proud of the boys – always am," she said.

She messaged Chris as he was getting the Lions ready for their preliminary final against Collingwood to tell him about Claremont's terrific start to their Grand Final.

She then realised Chris may have been otherwise occupied. "I Looked at my watch and thought, oh he's talking to the boys, but he didn't care," she said.

Beth presented the Fagan Medal that honours both Chris and Grant, to Grant as premiership winning coach.

The next week she was at the MCG for Chris's third successive Grand Final and saw him collect the Jock McHale medal, again, as winning coach. He also got a hug from his mother.

Chris gave his team medal to Jarrod Berry who missed the Grand Final through injury. The previous year he gave his Grand Final Medal to Oscar McInenery who missed that Grand Final, through injury.

Such selfless acts are what the Fagan family is all about.

Chris's wife Ursula also was on hand to give the premiership coach a hug. They've been married for 40 years and Ursula understands her husband better than anyone else (a possible exception would be his mother).

Ursula said: "He works extremely hard. What I find with Chris is when he is under a lot of pressure, he absolutely copes every time, and it is only afterwards that he feels the effects when he has got time to reflect. But when the crisis is on, in any particular aspect of his work, he just goes hard and gets through it.

"Whatever he needs and whatever he wants, I will always support him and I've always said that to him."

Ursula has always been there for Chris, even in the tough times – the health scares and the self-doubts. She has celebrated the successes, too.

They met at university in Tasmania when both were studying to be teachers.

They had similar values, even if their interests and personalities were different. Ursula loved the arts, while Chris was following his passion for sport, playing footy at the highest level in Tasmania.

"I didn't even follow football... I was more (into the arts)," Ursula said. "I enjoy it (football) now and I go to every game that I can.

"Our family has embraced the whole experience. I didn't come from a football background and I have certainly never sought a public life. It has been a little bit amusing (to see Chris become one of the game's most respected and recognised coaches), but we have met so many wonderful people. It has been pretty enjoyable, mostly."

In an interview with the *Herald Sun*, Ursula credited Chris's upbringing for of his work ethic and fierce determination as well as his loyalty and humility.

"I just know that he is very good at finding the next way forward, and I do think that is why they (the Lions) have been able to stay in the eight," she said.

"He is extremely good at his messaging. It is what a lot of teachers have got and what a lot of good coaches have got. They just have that ability to keep everyone on board and keep everyone headed in the right direction.

"The season always takes different turns and has highs and lows. A good coach will always keep his team heading in the right direction.

"Chris has enormous respect for all those boys and it is reciprocal and it makes it all the more meaningful. That's why I am so supportive of what Chris does because I can see the impact that he has on people but also the quality of life he creates for himself."

The Fagans arrived in Brisbane at a difficult time for the football club.

"When we first arrived I realised how vulnerable you are as the senior coach and how you have to keep your nerve," Ursula said.

"That's something Chris has been able to do. He is naturally an honest, open person with a really strong work ethic. And the two have combined beautifully. It has worked really well, because whenever things get a little bit uncertain or wobbly, you call on your core beliefs and your code of ethics and just keep going forward."

After family – including his children and grandchildren of course – there's another important person in Chris Fagan's corner.

Former Australian basketballer Phyl Smith, a four-times Olympian with the Boomers, has a behind-the-scenes role that cannot be understated though he's not in the public gaze. Smyth is a mentor and consultant, working closely with the coaching staff and particularly as a valuable sounding board for the head coach.

He's been described as the Lions "everything man" but colleagues describe his job as "keeping Fages sane."

South Australian Smyth joined the Lions in 2018 after a domestic career of 356 games at the top level of basketball as a point guard, playing for St Kilda, Canberra, Adelaide and Sydney. He was known as "The General" and was a premiership winner three times with the Canberra Boomers, then coach.

He usually sits in the Lions box on game day.

Fagan acknowledged that Smyth played a critical role in keeping him on track during the dark days of the racism controversy that engulfed key figures among the coaching hierarchy at Hawthorn from 2022, including Fagan.

"It's been a long two years for Chris," Smyth said back in 2024. It's so wrong; coaching alone will send you to dark places and then to pile that on top.

"It's a difficult time when things are being said about you that just aren't true and you can't defend yourself. But finally the rhetoric has changed," Smyth told 7 News.

"He's unique. He's a great person but also a genius with footy tactics," Smyth said of Fagan.

"People misread him, because he's got that father-like figure that the players love, they don't see the tactical genius behind it."

The racism controversy saw Fagan take a leave of absence from the club at the end of the 2020 season. But he soon realised they way to deal with things was to get back to work.

The Hawthorn issues were settled without adverse findings against Fagan.

The controversy was well behind the coach as the Lions set off along the road to back-to-back premierships.

When the talk came to the longer-term, Chris Fagan's name was tossed about for a role in the newest AFL team, the Tassie Devils.

The Devils were awarded a licence in 2023 and entered the VFL in 2026 and were to join the AFL in 2028.

But Fagan ruled himself out of a Devils role, stressing his commitment to Brisbane. He has said he wants to be remembered as a Brisbane Lions coach and did not think he would coach any other club.

The entry of the Devils was contingent on the construction of a new oval in Hobart, a condition that became a political "hot potato" until early December 2025 when the State Government approved the project estimated to cost $1 billion, a move Fagan supported.

Names of a potential coach of the team were still being bandied about as the year drew to a close.

Tasmanian Jeromey Webberley, who played 16 games with the Richmond Tigers in the early 2010s, was appointed coach of the VFL side ahead of the Devils' entry into the second-tier competition in 2026.

SCHOOLS OF THOUGHT

"If anyone wants to do a degree in teaching, I'd recommend it. There are so many spin-offs that come from it. Everything I learned as a teacher has helped me in my 27 years in footy, without a doubt."

That's the advice of Brisbane Lions premiership coach Chris Fagan.

When Lions CEO Greg Swann went looking for a new coach for the Brisbane Lions back in 2016, he was looking for someone who could educate players. He wanted someone who could restore relevance to the club that was struggling near the bottom of the ladder and reconnect with its young playing list.

The name Fagan, originally from Tasmania where he had been a teacher, was on Swann's list of "possibles." Fagan had not played in the elite levels of VFL/AFL but he was a highly regarded development coach, particularly for stints at Melbourne and Hawthorn.

His father had been a coach in Tasmania, so the young Fagan had early experience of seeing how a coach went about his job. When he was 21, he had his first real "go" at coaching – the team at his primary school.

After retiring as a player, he became an assistant coach at North Hobart, then head coach at Sandy Bay before taking over as Tassie Mariners coach in the national under-18 competition.

"I had always loved the teaching bit. I had always loved footy," Fagan had said.

"I thought: 'I've got a chance here to do the two things I love the most full-time.'

"I didn't do the Tassie Mariners job as a stepping stone to the AFL, I just wanted to do it.

"I probably thought I would do this a while and go back to teaching."

After spending 1995-98 as Mariners coach, Fagan saw that AFL clubs were appointing development coaches, so he sent his resume around. It came to the attention of Neale Daniher, coach of the Demons, who invited him to Melbourne.

"Finding Chris Fagan was the best recruiting decision I made in all my time at Melbourne," Daniher said.

Fagan coached Melbourne's reserves team in 1998-99, was an assistant to Daniher from 2000-04, and the club's football operations manager from 2005-07.

He then moved to Hawthorn, where he became an assistant coach then Head of Coaching and Development for almost a decade (2008-16).

Swann saw possibilities, so sounded out the 55-year-old.

Swann recalled: "The first thing Fages said to me was: 'I'm a coach, you know. I have coached a lot... I want to be an AFL coach.'"

Fagan's ability to educate players, communicate clearly, and nurture human development was central to his appeal. And that sealed the deal for him to be appointed head-coach at the Lions.

Fagan wasn't the only coach who branched out on a teaching career as a first step.

Robert Walls played for Carlton and Fitzroy during the 1960s and 1970s in the VFL. Through the 1980s and 1990s he coached in the VFL/AFL for 347 games with different clubs.

Walls was a Grade 6 teacher at Park Orchards Primary School around the time he was head coach at Fitzroy. (Walls passed away in May 2025).

David Parkin, a premiership captain and coach, also was a teacher. Leaving Toorak Teachers College, 21-year-old Parkin was posted to Monbulk Primary School east of Melbourne. He was assigned a class of 48 grade-three children.

That was in 1964, and he was in his fourth season with the Hawthorn Football Club. He was regarded as a tough and fearless "back-pocket specialist" and was appointed captain in 1969.

As captain, he led Hawthorn to their second premiership in 1971 and played 211 games for the club.

Parkin went to Western Australia and was captain-coach of Subiaco in 1975. He was back at Hawthorn as assistant coach under senior coach John Kennedy in 1976. Kennedy retired at the end of 1976 and Parkin was promoted to senior coach, bringing another premiership to the Hawks in 1978.

Moving to the coaching job at Carlton, he took the Blues to back-to-back premierships in 1981 and 1982.

Parkin then replaced Robert Walls as senior coach of Fitzroy when the clubs swapped coaches in 1986. He stayed with the Fitzroy Lions until 1988. Three years later he returned to Carlton, earning himself another premiership in 1995. He went back to Hawthorn in 2001 for two years as director of coaching.

According to Nine's *Footy Classified*, in 2021 when then on

Carlton's coaching sub-committee, Parkin tried to lure Fagan to the Blues as head coach. Panel member Caroline Wilson said: "Chris Fagan knocked that on the head immediately."

Parkin is considered one of the most influential coaches of the modern era and in 2002 was inducted into the Australian Football Hall of Fame.

Hawthorn had a couple of former teachers as fairly decent coaches: Alistair Clarkson and John Kennedy won seven premiership flags between them for the Hawks.

Brendon Bolton, also a qualified teacher (a Tasmanian, and Hall of Famer there) was head coach at Carlton from 2016-19. He was sacked after the club finished bottom of the ladder.

Bolton never played AFL. He played and coached in the Tasmanian Football League for North Hobart and Clarence, before arriving on the mainland to take up the top coaching job at VFL club Box Hill in 2009 before joining Hawthorn as an assistant where he had five games as interim coach in charge in 2014.

He went on to become director of coaching at Collingwood from 2016 and joined St Kilda as an assistant coach in 2024.

Some of the traits of a schoolteacher seem to match those of coaching: Discipline (minus the big stick and detention), adapting different styles, understanding students (players) and their specific needs, session plans, research and the ability to transfer knowledge.

The Sports Conflict Institute (SCI) is an organisation that has looked at the correlation between teaching and coaching.

On of their American experts noted: "Good coaches are able to motivate their pupils because they form deep relationships with them. Sometimes that does mean getting in someone's grill (it is America after all)... other times it means encouraging or putting your arms around a player. A good coach knows when to step in and when to step back. A good coach knows what buttons to push because she or he has an intimate relationship with the players. That is when the most effective classroom teaching occurs, too."

The AFL noted in 2023 that winds of change in coaching were blowing: "Look at the football departments across the 18 clubs, you will find 24 assistant or development coaches across the AFL – plus more analysts and coaches involved in the W programs – who have never played at the highest level."

Fagan told *AFL.com.au*: "There are a lot more blokes in AFL footy that haven't had that traditional background compared to when I started. It was reasonably rare when Neale Daniher gave me a job back in 1998. Coaching staffs then were three people, so things have changed a fair bit, and it has evolved a fair bit which has allowed people from non-traditional backgrounds to get more opportunities."

Are there similarities between coaching and teaching?

Chris Fagan: "Coaching is just like teaching, really, it's just that your classroom is full of footballers and you've got it all year round and you look after their development not just as footballers but as people. That is fundamentally what you do as a schoolteacher."

He told the *Herald Sun*: "In teaching (and in coaching) you need to build relationships with people and understand them, to get the best out of them. Encourage them to take risks and have a growth mindset. Develop an environment built on trust and safety.

"You need to be highly organised. The management skills you learn as a teacher help as a coach and in life in general.

"If anyone wants to do a degree in teaching, I'd recommend it. There are so many spin-offs that come from it. Everything I learned as a teacher has helped me in my 27 years in footy, without a doubt."

Who influenced him to take a path towards teaching and ultimately coach footballers?

His social science teacher, Bronwyn Sidebottom, a surname name coincidentally familiar in AFL circles, was one person who influenced Fagan's development.

He still keeps in touch with Mrs Sidebottom.

"I can't thank her enough and she knows that because I've said that to her many times," he said.

Fagan regards some of the favours he does as payback for all the people who had helped him throughout his life. They included a couple of his high school teachers in Queenstown, and Mrs Sidebottom.

"The general course of your life if you were born in that town was: You went to school, and then you went and got an apprenticeship in the mine, and then you worked in the mine for the rest of your life and stayed in Queenstown," he said in an interview with *The Age*.

"But I had a couple of teachers in high school who sort of said to me, 'Well, not that there is anything wrong with doing that, but if you are interested in doing other things or going to university, you have got the capacity to do it'.

"So, I always look back on them and think that was a bit of a watershed moment for me because I was probably just thinking I was going to do what everybody else does in that town, and then I changed my mind and set myself to go to university and get a Bachelor of Education (degree).

"It was a bit of a sliding door moment. That's an example, I guess, probably the most profound example in my life, of a couple of teachers helping me out."

THE COACH'S TEAM

When it comes to putting together a premiership team, recruitment staff play an important role in configuring a squad for the coach to mould into a team of champions.

Most club recruiters generally have a low profile until trading season when contracts are offered and players can move to a new club.

According to the AFL, no AFL/VFL premiership team has ever played together again in its entirety after claiming a flag.

In the case of the Lions before 2025, the four-person recruiting team was faced with covering for a possible loss of six listed free agents; one restricted and five unrestricted.

The Lions' list was managed by Dom Ambrogio, Steve Conole, Shane Rogers and Leon Harris, names not particularly well-known to anybody outside the club.

Ambrogio was appointed as list manager in February 2017, Chris Fagan's first year at the helm. The Lions "won" the wooden spoon that year, but it was the beginning of a long road to the top.

In eight seasons since then, the Lions played in seven finals series (2019-2025), three successive Grand Finals and back-to-back premierships, a credit to Fagan, obviously, but also to Ambrogio, Conole, Rogers and Harris who have played key roles in the progression to successive premierships.

Of the 48 players on the Lions' list in 2017, only eight were there in 2025: Harris Andrews, Dayne Zorko, Hugh McCluggage, Darcy Gardiner, Oscar McInerney and Ryan Lester, who all contributed to glory on the last day in September while injuries meant Jarrod Berry and Eric Hipwood were sidelined.

Leon Harris probably is the better known of the recruiting "gang of four."

Harris played for Fitzroy in the VFL from 1979 to 1989, as a rover/midfielder for 186 senior appearances and 100 goals. He represented Victoria at the 1988 Bicentennial Carnival.

After retiring, he coached in the VFA/VFL and later worked in junior football development then player recruitment. He also mentored young players. His brother, Bernie, played for Fitzroy, the Brisbane Bears, and St Kilda.

He joined the Lions as a recruitment consultant before the 2017 season.

Ambrogio spent more than 15 years in the recruiting departments of the Gold Coast Suns and Western Bulldogs before joining Brisbane.

Steve Conole, a former manager with the Oakleigh Chargers in the Victorian Under 18s Talent League, joined the Lions at the start of 2011 and has been recruiting manager for Brisbane since 2014.

Talent scout Shane Rogers is a former national recruiting manager for Carlton. He joined the Lions as a recruiting co-ordinator at the end of 2015 and has been a pro scout since the end of 2018.

Other key players in recruitment, particularly with clubs based outside Melbourne, are the talent scouts whose job it is to identify potential stars.

For example, Lions pro scout Andrew Farrell has been based in Melbourne and has been responsible for watching matches in the Victorian Football League (VFL) and Australian Football League (AFL), as well as assessing players from other state leagues including the South Australian National Football League (SANFL) and Western Australian Football League (WAFL).

The Brisbane Lions have a network of part-time scouts stationed interstate, covering the key Australian football regions in Victoria, South Australia, Western Australia, Tasmania, and NSW/ACT.

This allows the club to identify players outside its own academy zone. The scouts can also help the club secure mature-age or ready-made recruits from interstate.

The Lions do not disclose the number of scouts on their books, but reports suggest there are four part-time scouts in Victoria, three in South Australia, two in Western Australia, and one each in Tasmania and NSW/ACT – at least 11 part-time interstate scouts.

Coaching an AFL team isn't a one-person job and Chris Fagan has a team of assistants that he has acknowledged.

"I'm part of a committed team of coaches and support staff at the Lions who strive to deliver a high-quality program on a daily basis to bring out the best in our players," Fagan said in response to being awarded the Alan Jeans Trophy in 2025 as the AFL Coaches Association of the Coach of the Year for the third time.

"The energy and expertise that our coaches bring to their roles has been pivotal to our consistency and success as a team.

I know it's my name that goes on the trophy, but in reality, it's the work of the coaching group that matters most and so I accept this award on behalf of everyone who works in our Football Department at the Lions.

"I also want to recognise and thank the players for their efforts. The main responsibility for performance sits on their shoulders. The players at the Lions are great characters and committed professionals who make our job as coaches so enjoyable and rewarding."

The Brisbane Lions' assistant coaches for the 2025 AFL season included Stuart Dew, Cameron Bruce, Dale Morris, and Ben Hudson. There were some Hawthorn connections among them, probably a factor in them joining Fagan's team.

Midfield coach Cam Bruce was named AFLCA Assistant Coach of the Year in 2025, beating Adelaide's Murray Davis and Lions defensive coach Dale Morris.

Stuart Dew: Appointed as forwards coach in 2025, joining the club after a period as part-time specialist coach during the successful 2024 premiership campaign. Dew played for Adelaide and Hawthorn in the AFL and joined Brisbane after being moved on in 2023 after coaching the Gold Coast. Dew went to Port Adelaide at the end of 2025.

Cameron Bruce: Midfield coach, recognised as the 2025 AFL Coaches Association Assistant Coach of the Year for his impact on the Lions' midfield and stoppage structures. Bruce played for Melbourne and Hawthorn in the AFL.

Dale Morris: Assistant coach with a focus on backs, commended for his contributions to the defensive coaching group. Morris spent his playing career at the Western Bulldogs and was in a premiership-winning team there.

Ben Hudson: Assistant coach, experienced in ruck and defensive skills, and has developmental coaching roles. Hudson's playing career saw him at Adelaide, Western Bulldogs, Brisbane and Collingwood.

The Lions' general manager of football is Danny Daly, responsible for football operations.

He joined the club in 2014 and spent six seasons on the Club's coaching panel, including four years as Fagan's right-hand man and head of strategy. He was appointed general manager of football in 2022.

Across 20 years in the AFL industry he worked as opposition scout and welfare manager to a range of various coaching positions. He previously had been at Collingwood, North Melbourne and Richmond in the AFL.

It was no surprise to learn late in 2025 that the Gold Coast was keen to lure him a little further south after Wayne Campbell took up a position with the Sydney academy.

Daly had been much sought-after; he fielded approaches from West Coast and Melbourne to apply for their senior coaching positions, and Collingwood reportedly was interested in getting him as football boss.

Daly spurned the approaches and said he was staying with the Lions. He took over from David Noble at the Lions at the end of the 2020 season.

On game day you can usually see Chris Fagan sitting on the interchange bench with players, wearing a headset. He is in constant contact with the coach's box in the stands where you most likely will find Daly passing on information, including reports from assistant coaches.

The players seem to appreciate Fagan being at ground level where he can give instant feedback while Daly filters tactical information from above as assistant coaches report in. This structure is credited with strengthening the connection between the coaching group and the playing group.

Brisbane wasn't resting on its laurels with its coaching team. There were notable changes for 2026.

The line-up:

Chris Fagan – Senior Coach

Dale Morris – Assistant Coach (Defence)

Cameron Bruce – Assistant Coach (Midfield)

Daniel Lloyd – Assistant Coach (Forwards)

Scott Borlace – Head of Development

Ben Hudson – VFL Coach

Liam Jones – Development Coach

Scott Thompson – Development Coach

Daniel Lloyd was promoted to assistant coach (forwards) after spending the past two years as a development coach with the Lions.

Lloyd, who played 101 AFL games with GWS before retiring and starting his coaching career with the Lions, replaced Stuart Dew as forwards coach.

The Club appointed former Western Bulldogs defender Liam Jones and former Adelaide Crows midfielder Scott Thompson as development coaches.

Jones, who played 205 games with Carlton and the Western Bulldogs, was starting his coaching journey with the Lions.

The 34-year-old is seen as good fit in the development role, just coming off the Western Bulldogs AFL list.

Thompson started his coaching career in 2017 as a development coach with Port Adelaide. He played 308 games with Melbourne and Adelaide.

After a break from the AFL, Thompson coached Unley in Division 2 of the Adelaide Football League.

Lions General Manager Football Danny Daly said the Club was thrilled by all three appointments.

Dayne Frew was appointed Head of the Youi Brisbane Lions Academy, to oversee the club's talent development pathway.

Frew joins the Academy with over 20 years experience in talent and coaching roles, having recently been Regional Talent Manager Sunshine Coast / Wide Bay for the past five years.

His background is in high-performance football programs, player development, and leadership. He is also experienced in identifying emerging talent.

The coaching team faced the extra challenge of dealing with significant rule changes for the 2026 season, including the restart of play with the end of centre-bounces just one of changes that would impact the role of key players, notably ruckmen.

Also, the removal of the substitute provision meant clubs would name 23 players, five of them on the interchange bench, with the type of player chosen for that role needing careful consideration. The substitute rule proved so valuable to the Lions in the 2025 Grand Final when Chris Fagan sent Lachie Neale on to the field late for an immediate impact, something that riled Geelong coach Chris Scott, although he was quick to deny his dissatisfaction with the substitute system was a case of "sour grapes."

Getting players au fait with the rule changes would be the job of club coaches, with some help from umpires, as Greg Swann from the AFL put it: "The players will adjust to it." Having been not long coming out of a club (the Lions) he observed "It's amazing how quickly they do adjust to whatever rule changes. The coaches drum it into them. We have umpires come out and practise it."

Summary of 2026 AFL Rule Changes

Boundary and kick-in rules

A "last disposal out of bounds" free kick will apply between the 50-metre arcs: if the ball goes out from a disposal, a free is paid against the last player to dispose. Insufficient intent will still apply inside the 50m.

Players taking a kick-in after a behind now have about eight seconds to play on or kick, bringing kick-ins into line with the existing eight-second guideline for marks and frees.

Centre and ruck contests

The centre bounce is being removed; the ball will be thrown up to restart play.

At centre ball-ups, a ruck cannot cross the centre circle line and make body contact with the opposing ruck before the contest; around the ground, umpires can restart play without formal ruck nominations, though "third man up" remains illegal.

Positioning and "stand" rule

The 6-6-6 formation remains, but teams are no longer required to have a player starting in the goal square at centre ball-ups.

Any player within five metres of the mark (the protected area) when a mark or free is paid must stand; backing out to get "outside five" from inside that zone is no longer allowed and will be more strictly penalised.

Tackling interpretations

A deliberate shrug in a tackle will be treated as prior opportunity, similar to a fend-off or other evasive move, making it easier for umpires to call holding the ball when the player is then correctly tackled.

Interchange

The substitute rule has been scrapped in favour of a five-player interchange bench.

Tribunal and conduct tweaks

For 2026, stomach punches are proposed to be graded up to "medium impact," meaning a one-match ban rather than just a fine, and there is a push to ban visible unofficial sponsorships or offensive symbols on gear or skin.

Low-level fines are proposed to escalate only for repeat offences of the same type, and the match review officer will have a more discretion in grading some high-contact incidents.

Brisbane's football support staff include performance and wellbeing managers; a physical performance coach; head physiotherapist; high performance manager; rehabilitation coach; sports performance dietitian; opposition and football analyst; and a sports trainer.

The CEO responsible for the running of the club until 2025 was Greg Swann and much of the club's success in getting Fagan and his team together can be attributed to him.

Swann previously held CEO roles with the Carlton and Collingwood clubs. Little wonder the AFL sought him out for the role of Executive General Manager of Football Performance back in Melbourne. Swann was replaced at Brisbane by Sam Graham to oversee club business and administration.

According to the AFL, a typical club generally operates with about 8-12 ancillary staff focused on training, running, and medical support, all within an overall football department team of approximately 25 people, the maximum permitted in each club who can have physical contact with players.

AFL clubs are required to have, at a minimum, an accredited sports trainer or qualified medical professional present for all matches and training.

Those ancillary roles such as trainers, runners, and medical personnel, usually comprise 1 or 2 doctors; 3 physiotherapists (one often acting mainly as a masseur); 5 high performance/sports science staff (who often include trainers and conditioning personnel); there are also roles for psychologists, player development managers, and compliance managers.

AFL club travelling parties for interstate games usually range from 30 to 50 personnel, including medical and conditioning teams, analysts, team managers, operations, media, and security in addition to on-field runners and trainers.

The total of employees at the Brisbane Lions in 2025 was almost 300 on top of the football department, including all business, administration, and other operational roles.

Andrew Wellington is club chairman. He is also chair of Queensland Rail. His background is in accounting and commerce, including corporate governance.

Directors are Cathie Reid, Chris Johnson, Cyril Jinks, Dean Gibson, Sarah Kelly, Mick Power, Tim Forrester, Maxine Horne and previous Lions three-peat premiership coach (2001-2003), Leigh Mathews.

Matthews, an AFL legend, has praised Chris Fagan for transforming the Brisbane Lions into a consistent premiership contender and reflected positively on the club's progress under his leadership.

What influenced Fagan's coaching style?

"The best coaches I had were the ones that built relationships with me. I felt like I would want to do more for them and sacrifice more for them than the coaches that just saw you as a player that could help them win a game of football," was Fagan's answer.

There's no shame in taking on a team that contends for the wooden spoon. For starters, the only way is up. Fagan's two premierships so far could become a repeat of what happened in 1999 when the Lions appointed Leigh Matthews. At that point the Lions had won the wooden-spoon with a 5-1-17 record the previous season. There was turmoil on and off the field.

Matthews took the Lions to three premierships in succession before standing down at the end of the 2008 season. They returned to the finals in 2009 when they finished sixth, but lean seasons followed, 12th their best result (2013 – 10 wins) from 2010 to 2018.

The Lions collected another wooden spoon in 2017, but Fagan plotted a course out of the backwater. Now they have two premierships, back-to-back. No one could rule out a three-peat.

TRUE GRIT

PLAYER WAS LOST IN THE MUD
City footballers and supporters who visited and played a combined team at Queenstown will never again complain about the elements of the York Park oval. The Redlegs experienced a real "West Coaster," with a hailstorm thrown in for good measure. The gravel playing area is a paradise compared to early days when it was "button grass" and mud. During a match in the long ago, a hardcore by-stander was seen scratching in the mud with a stick. When asked what he was doing, he replied "I saw two players go down there, but only one came up."

A report in the *Sunday Evening Examiner,* Launceston, 22 October 1849, that goes some way to explaining why 'The Gravel' at Queenstown became a preferable playing surface to mud and grass.

There are a couple of Queenstown locals who can tell more tales than most people about "The Gravel" that is the town's football oval.

Everyone who has played football there can talk about The Gravel, many fondly but maybe not those who still bear the scars.

Chris Fagan probably knows quite a bit about it, too. It is where he cut his teeth (and probably several other body parts) in the world of football.

Fagan has good memories: "I lived the first 15 years of my

life around there and I loved every minute of it."

The Gravel Oval at Queenstown, Tasmania, was built in 1895 and football has been played there for around 130 years, at least since 1896. It is one of the oldest continuously used football ovals in Tasmania.

But why gravel?

Gravel was chosen because the heavy-metal pollution from the nearby Mt Lyell copper mine and the region's high annual rainfall made it almost impossible to maintain a grass playing field. Gravel was chosen to prevent fields turning into unusable muddy quagmires and fend off possible loss of players!

For all who have played football there, gravel rash was a badge of honour, of sorts.

The first official league based on The Gravel (aka The Gravel Oval, Queenstown Oval, The Rec) in 1924, was the Queenstown Football Association.

It was succeeded by the Western Tasmanian Football Association (WTFA) and comprised mostly miners living and working on the State's West Coast. (In the 1920s, Tasmania's West Coast mining industry centred on copper production at Mount Lyell, near Queenstown, alongside silver-lead and tin operations that were declining.)

Of all the clubs from the WTFA competition, only Queenstown Football Club (formerly the Blues, most recently the Crows) and Rosebery-Toorak Football Club remain. They now take part in competitions on the Northwest Coast conducted by the Darwin Football Association (formed in 1951). DFA has covered the region since the WTFA closed in 1993 and is the only league in Australia that plays games on a gravel surface. The Queenstown Crows joined the league in 1994 and were premiers in 2024 but lost to the South Burnie Hawks in the 2025 Grand Final.

Queenstown Football Club was formed in 1977 by the merger of the Smelters Football Club (a link to the local industry) and the City Football Club. The Gravel was and still is Queenstown's home ground. Chris Fagan's father Austin played and coached the Smelters team. His uncle Gerald also played for Smelters Robins in the WTFAL.

Austin Fagan also was captain-coach of Gormanston.

Chris Fagan played for Lyell-Gormanston after the amalgamation of the two teams and, aged 15, he played in the senior premiership.

He first set foot on the Gravel as a player, in the Under 13s. But he saw plenty of football there as he watched his father at work as the coach.

For almost a century, the ground served as the Grand Final venue for the WTFA.

An annual rainfall of 2,408mm on the West Coast ensures the surface isn't always rock-hard. A heavy (10-tonne) roller is used to flatten the gravel to create a consistent playing area and it requires regular replenishment of the gravel, 6-10 truckloads a year.

Also, abrasions must be well-treated to avoid the risk of infection.

Brett Schulze and Cheryl Gamble have seen more of the gravel and its effects than most.

Brett Schulze is a Queenstown chap "born and bred" and few people know better than the almost 500-game West Coast legend

"The Gravel" home of the Queenstown Crows, Mt Lyell, Tasmania.

Source: We Are Explorers

about the grit it takes to play on gravel.

Schulze, 60, played his first game there as a 16-year-old on-baller in 1978. Chris Fagan had left Queenstown by then, aged 17, but some of his blood may well have been embedded in the gravel.

Now an almost 500-game veteran of football in the area, Brett Schulze has known the ground since he was a "little tacker."

He knew the ground well by the time he played his first game, for Lyell-Gormanston against Queenstown. "I wasn't so nervous about the gravel because we grew up with it and running around on it when we were kids," he said.

"My dad Max was a ruckman for Gormanston, so we'd all come along to the footy on a Sunday. That's when footy was played back then and it was a big day out."

Of all the grounds he played at, Queenstown was the toughest to deal with, Schulze told James Bresneha of the *Hobart Mercury*.

"You'd lose skin, you could never doubt that you'll always lose skin playing out here in every single game," he said.

The trick was to avoid "the slide".

"You have got to learn to roll more than slide," he said.

"If you slide then the bark comes off. After a while you don't think anything of it. It stings for a few days, every time you get in the shower, and then it starts to come right."

Brett Schulze later played for the Queenstown Crows before going to Penguin. He returned to Queenstown to coach the Crows from 2004 to 2009, including premiership glory.

Cheryl Gamble saw another side to The Gravel. She took on the role of Queenstown Crows team manager in 1999.

Doing the laundry every Saturday night was just as arduous a task as tending to gravel rash after a match, she told the *Launceston Examiner*.

She knew a fair bit about that task after 25 years of service to the club. Every week she washed 42 guernseys, often covered in mud. And there were usually some blood stains, too.

"On a wet day you have to hose them off first," she said. Back in the day before facility upgrades, the players probably had to be hosed off, too.

But the guernseys were Cheryl Gamble's main job back then.

"After a game I usually soaked them in some buckets on my back decking, and then I washed them the next day," she said.

"The guernseys now are a lot easier than what they were years ago; they're that nice stretchy material now, they're a lot easier. Back then they were that thicker material, so they were a lot harder to clean. I'd sooner play on the gravel than I would at Natone and Yolla, which is cow paddock. It's not so much bloody guernseys but muddy guernseys. I would say they were the two worst grounds that you would have to go to."

Her roles at the club were extended to cleaning up the dressing room, recording player statistics for the reserves and the seniors, acting as an interchange steward, working the canteen and operating the bar. Oh, and 12-years as club secretary.

Life membership at the Crows and of the Darwin Football Association would seem to have been well-earned.

The 2025 season was her last as the full-time team manager. Filling in for a short time became more than a quarter-century commitment.

"It's been a long haul but I am done, I've got three

grandkids, my two eldest play basketball and my granddaughter's been away with the Tassie sides for the last couple of years," Cheryl Gamble said.

"I miss Saturdays... the little fella, he plays on Saturday but I never get to see him play."

Chris Fagan had not forgotten the people of Queenstown where he spent his early years, and they had not forgotten him.

After winning the 2024 AFL premiership, Fagan took the Cup to Queenstown. His brother Grant was along for the ride.

Locals had celebrated Chris Fagan's premiership at the Queenstown Golf Club, where the toasts to their "local hero" no doubt flowed freely.

When he arrived there on a weekend late in November 2024 it marked a much-delayed homecoming for Fagan. The locals turned up in droves.

Fagan said it was the first time he had seen the now heritage-listed Gravel in more than two decades.

"People sort of talk about this place that they haven't been to, like we're all Martians," he said. "We're actually normal people, good people. And that's what I experienced in my time here."

Fagan said he loved the town when he was a kid – there was plenty of sport to be had – footy, cricket, basketball were all options.

"I was a bit of a swimmer as well, believe it or not," he said.

"I could play all the sport that I wanted to play. It was always about five minutes away, so Mum and Dad didn't have to take me too far to the oval."

He was only too happy to take the Cup back to Queenstown. He also visited the patients at the local hospital, pupils at St

Joseph's Primary School and the museum. A junior football clinic followed with coaches from AFL Tasmania taking part under the watchful eye of the premiership coach. He took a Q and A session in the Queenstown Crows clubrooms.

More than two decades since he last visited The Gravel, Fagan said: "It's funny to stand on it.

"I reckon it's actually not a bad surface.

"It was good to see it again. I learned not to fall over here at this ground because of the gravel."

There had been some changes of course. The cement cycle track around the outside of the ground was gone, for reasons of safety.

"If you landed on your head in the bike track you'd be in all sorts of trouble," Fagan said, "But it looks funny without it around the ground because that's how I remember it.

"Some of the changerooms are still here and some have disappeared, and there are a lot more trees on the hill than there used to be."

Fagan said the ground wasn't as bad as it looked.

"There's a lot of rainfall around here and turf turns into mud pretty quickly, so the gravel stands up in all conditions... it makes a lot of sense.

"People carry on like it's full of sharp stones but it's a very sandy gravel so it's not that bad," he said.

"It's a bit hard on footballs and a bit hard on moulded-sole boots. The stops do wear down pretty quickly."

The ground doesn't quite meet the standards for the surface for grounds laid down by the AFL – "A ground must be grassed, have a minimum length of 135 metres and a minimum width of

110 metres."

Obviously an exemption was required at Queenstown, at least as far as the surface was concerned.

The Tasmanian Football Hall of Fame recognised the importance of the ground and in 2007 included it in its list of notable facets of football in the state.

A handful of top Australian rules footballers grew up in Queenstown, as well as Chris Fagan. Collingwood premiership captain Sid Coventry, Sydney Swans player Daryn Cresswell, the late Carlton player Arthur Hodgson and St Kilda and Richmond legend Ian Stewart began their football careers there.

The Gravel may help explain their toughness.

Stewart was born in Queenstown and learnt to play on the gravel before moving to Hobart when he was in his teens.

"I still have scars," the triple Brownlow Medallist said.

Jamie Cooper's painting, "Tasmania's Team of the Century", shows gravel visible on the knees of Stewart.

Stewart says the gravel taught him not to fall over – "That's why the Tasmanians seem to have very good balance."

Aaron Burden, 300-game veteran for the Queenstown Crows: "My knees are pretty knocked up, but you learn to roll with it, or land on someone, or stay on your feet."

Famed historian Geoffrey Blainey wrote the social and mining history of Queenstown, *The Peaks of Lyell* (Melbourne University Press). He also played football on the Gravel, for Smelters.

Born in Victoria, his team was Geelong and one of his regrets was missing a trip back to the mainland for Geelong's appearances in Grand Finals in the early 1950s. In 1953, he was playing in a Grand Final of his own in Tasmania while Geelong lost to Collingwood.

Blainey first played football for the Smelters club in 1951, but not for the whole season. He was a regular in 1952 and 1953. He kicked 24 goals in his last season and scored four goals in the Queenstown association B grade Grand Final victory over Gormanston (a replay after a draw first time round). Newspaper reports noted A. Fagan was a teammate.

Blainey also served on the club committee for a year.

Prof. Blainey referred to The Gravel in a memoir for *Gravel & Mud: An Anthology of Football in the Mountains of Western Tasmania* by John Carswell, Tony Newport, Chris Carswell for Lake Press.

"It was just about the most dangerous football ground in the whole world of Australian Rules," he wrote. "The surface was as hard on a rainy as on a sunny day, but it did have the big advantage that it was not boggy or slippery even during the wettest of winters.

"If you were pushed in the back and fell suddenly, the likely result was gravel rash or blood. Many of the experienced players learned to hunch their body an instant before their upper arm or shoulder hit the hard ground. Wisely, nearly all the footballers wore long sleeves and long socks throughout the year.

"Of course, football boots had to be altered to fit the gravel surface. As some pieces of gravel were rather large and pointed, especially after the oval had just received fresh loads of gravel, a drop-kick or stab-kick could be risky. The punt kick was generally favoured."

Blayney, a freelance writer at the time, spent three years in

Queenstown writing the history of the Mount Lyell Mining Company. *The Peaks of Lyell* was published in 1954.

Football teams that arose from the Mt Lyell mine over various eras included Smelters (also known as the Robins for their bright red jumpers), Miners, Flux, Mechanics and Railways.

Over time at least 12 football teams called The Gravel home. A siren was borrowed from the Mt Lyell Mines to signal the start and end of each quarter.

Since 1895, The Gravel oval has also hosted cricket and athletics. These days it is also a tourist attraction.

A recent post on *Trip Advisor*: "Really interesting to see a gravel oval but it's clear to see why, noting the rainfall this area gets and how they've overcome this to building this sporting ground. Worth visiting to understand the history and check it out."

A MEASURE OF THE MAN

Chris Fagan walked an entire lap of the MCG after the 2025 Grand Final to make sure he thanked all the fans

In 2017, Fagan and recruiting manager Stephen Conole travelled around the country to personally welcome that year's new recruits.

Without wishing to sound like a nomination for sainthood, the selflessness of Chris Fagan should be noted. His career has always been typified by selfless acts – both symbolic and substantial – and reveal a leadership style grounded in empathy, humility, and a genuine concern for his players.

Two selfless acts involving Grand Final medals awarded to premiership coach Chris Fagan, brought out to those who didn't already know him, the side of the man who has become much loved in Brisbane.

His benevolence involved two players who missed Grand Final glory – Jarrod Berry in 2025 and Oscar McInenery in 2024.

Oscar McInerney was the 2024 Grand Final's heart-break story, missing the decider after suffering a shoulder injury.

But Chris Fagan didn't forget his much-admired ruckman, giving him the coach's Grand Final medal.

McInerney played in all but one game in the 2024 season.

“You get the Jock McHale medal for being the premiership coach and then I got handed one of the medals the players got, and I thought, what am I getting handed this for I’m not a player,” Fagan explained to *Fox Footy*.

“I had the medal and checked that it wasn’t a mistake, that they hadn’t given it to me by accident; it wasn’t, and I made the decision to give it to Oscar, it seemed fair.”

Fagan said he gave the medal to McInerney on the Thursday after the Grand Final and chose to do it during a team meeting, rather than at the best-and-fairest awards.

“It was a very popular thing – a big cheer went up and he was pretty happy to accept it,” Fagan said.

Fagan didn’t forget the big man a year later after he’d won a Grand Final medal in his own right, then opted to retire.

McInerney was selected with Pick 37 in the 2016 rookie draft. He called time on his career in 2025 just a week after helping the Club claim back-to-back premierships.

The 31-year-old had to work hard for his AFL dream to come true, playing for Montrose in Melbourne’s Eastern Football League then the Casey Demons in the VFL.

From there he not only became one of the competition’s leading ruckmen, but a cult figure at the Lions and throughout the AFL. In the end, a back injury helped him make up his mind to retire.

An emotional tribute to him was a letter written by Chris Fagan and posted on the club’s website:

Dear Oscar,

Last Thursday when I asked you whether you were intending to retire, in typical Oscar style you evaded giving me an answer.

I wanted to know because the Club Champion Awards were on that night and if you were going to retire, I wanted to be able to say a few words about you and the positive influence you have had on our club in the nine seasons that you have played for us.

I should have known what you were up to – evading giving me an answer because you didn't want me to make a fuss about you on the big night.

Just wanting to slip out the door quietly, riding off into the sunset with no fanfare or accolades.

You sent me a text at 10.01am the next day asking if I had some time to catch up with you.

"Hi Fages – just seeing if you've got any spare time in your calendar today... I can be anywhere, Springfield if you're out there, Bulimba, wherever. If you've got a spare minute, I would be really grateful. No pressure though – if you're busy it can slide through to the keeper, and I can just give you a call down the track. Thank you."

I texted you back saying I could catch you at my place in Bulimba at 1.30pm.

I was pretty sure you were coming to tell me that your time was up. You didn't let me down.

I re-read the text that you sent me that morning and it very much sums you up.

Didn't want to intrude on my time, prepared to meet me at a time and place that suited me and even offering to 'let it through to the keeper" if I was too busy.

One of the biggest decisions you've ever made in your life, and you made it all about me!

This is so typical of you Oscar, always putting others before yourself and your needs. Humble, low maintenance and thoughtful to the end.

Well, I decided to write this letter to you and put it on the club website so that the general public can understand the great team man that you are.

For me I will never forget the sacrifice that you made for the team in the 2024 Preliminary Final against Geelong.

You dislocated your shoulder early in that match but returned to the field with it strapped up and gave us another 40 minutes of football before it popped out again, ending any chance that you had of playing in the Grand Final the following week if we were fortunate enough to beat the Cats, which we did.

That 40 minutes meant we didn't have to use our sub too early in the game and save Joe Daniher from having to spend an extended period in the ruck.

You were in considerable pain and discomfort, yet you pushed on for as long as you could.

The next week on Grand Final day you sat on the interchange bench, constantly offering encouragement and advice to your teammates as they came on and off the field.

When the siren sounded and we won the game your happiness for your teammates was unbridled and incredibly genuine.

No sadness because you missed out just pure unadulterated joy and excitement for your mates. It's an image and moment I will never forget.

We are all so happy for you that you got to play in a winning Grand Final against the Cats this year.

You did so carrying a back injury that would stop most players from taking the field.

Your sheer will power to contribute to the victory and help your teammates carried you through.

It was so good for all of us to see the joy on your face as you ran up on stage to receive your premiership medallion after the final siren had sounded.

A career complete with a premiership victory.

We will miss you "Big O" – everything you did at our club was for the benefit of the team.

You played 165 games and in every one of them you gave your best possible effort.

Over a nine-year career you've played against and beaten some of the great ruckmen in the AFL.

You worked hard on the track and did everything you could to maximise your talent.

You can leave the game with no regrets, loved and admired by your teammates and respected by your opponents.

Well done big fella – we will miss you. - Fages

OSCAR McINERNEY

Oscar McInerney was born on 10 July 1994 and attended Ringwood Secondary College in Melbourne's east, graduating in 2012.

After leaving school, he played local football for Montrose in the Eastern Football League. He was recruited to VFL club Casey Scorpions for 2016, as a 204 cm ruckman.

He won the A Todd Medal for the best player in the AFL Victoria Development League and featured in the Scorpions' VFL Finals campaign and attended the NAB AFL State Combine.

He was drafted by Brisbane with pick 37 in the 2017 rookie draft and was part of the Lions' NEAFL (reserves) premiership in 2017 when they defeated Sydney by 3 points.

McInerney made his AFL debut for the Lions in a loss to Greater

Western Sydney at Sydney Showground Stadium in Round 6 of the 2018 season. He had seven disposals, nine hit-outs and made three tackles.

He was a member of Brisbane's 2025 premiership side, after missing the 2024 Grand Final win due to injury. He announced his retirement eight days after the 2025 Grand Final, after 165 games.

Chris Fagan didn't write him a letter but spoke in high praise of Jarrod Berry who missed the 2025 Grand Final through injury.

Fagan supported Berry as he made the difficult choice to rule himself out in the interests of the team in case his shoulder failed again. The coach commended him for putting the club's success above his personal dream of playing in the decider.

Berry featured in 24 games for the Lions in 2025, unfortunately suffering the same fate as Oscar McInerney, dislocating his shoulder during a Preliminary Final victory.

Berry, who had a premiership medal from the previous year, tried to prove his fitness before selection of the team, but had further issues with his shoulder at training and was omitted.

Berry's absence was used as motivation by his teammates, his number and photo displayed in the rooms for inspiration.

Fagan spoke about the midfielder's influence during the club's successful campaign.

Berry was consistently among the best for the Lions through thick and thin throughout the 2024 and 2025 seasons, and signed up at least until 2029.

He was recognised as the 2025 Robert Flower Wingman of the Year for his consistent tough, hard-nosed play both defensively and offensively, averaging around 20 disposals per game with strong defensive pressure acts (7.4 per game), marks, and inside-50 contributions. His versatility and work rate were highlighted as key assets for coach Fagan throughout the season. Berry averaged almost 20 disposals per game in 2025 (12.1 kicks and 7.8 handballs).

Fagan paid a heartfelt tribute to Jarrod Berry in the changerooms by presenting him with his own premiership medal, an act recognising Berry's contributions throughout the season and his heartbreak at missing the big game.

Fagan handed Berry the medal in front of his teammates, continuing his tradition of honouring sidelined players who played a significant role in the campaign.

Another selfless moment involved his handling of Dayne Zorko's captaincy in 2023. Fagan gave Zorko the dignity of deciding for himself when to step down as captain, even though it would have been easier for the coach to make the call. He described this as part of building a "selfless" team culture that prioritises respect and trust.

Zorko revealed after the 2024 Grand Final victory that Chris Fagan had promised him he could lift the premiership trophy if the team won a Grand Final. The coach kept his word.

Zorko was captain from 2018 to 2022.

"Me and Fages came on this journey... we experienced the lows and the highs (together)," Zorko said after the match.

"Fages came up to me and said: 'You're going up on stage, and you deserve this more than anyone.'

"I'm so honoured that he allowed me to get up there and hold the cup with those two absolute legends (Lachie Neale and Harris Andrews).

"He actually promised me about two years ago when I handed the captaincy over and said 'if we ever win it, you'll be the first person up there'. He stuck by his word on that, and that's the sort of guy he is."

Instead of having one hand on the cup as it was raised, Fagan gave the honour to his leadership men and stood to the side until the players spotted him and brought him into the celebrations.

In 2024 Fagan paid a special tribute to Joe Daniher. Daniher missed the Lions' unsuccessful tilt at the premiership decider in 2023, but got a deserved medal a year later in the winning side before announcing his retirement.

Fagan probably had an inkling that Daniher's retirement might be coming. Daniher had told him the previous year he would retire if the Lions beat Collingwood in the Grand Final. The near-miss meant there was unfinished business. He earned his premiership medallion a year later.

Fagan described Daniher as a "special player" and thought that he could have played for another five years.

Chris Fagan introduced Daniher at the Brisbane Lions' Best and Fairest event at season's end: "You've given us so many wonderful moments and crazy moments and head-scratching moments, and all those moments, but we'll never forget you, mate, you've been so good for our footy club."

Clearly Fagan held Daniher in high regard and respected his decision to retire on his own terms.

Joe Daniher's speech focused on thanking two specific groups.

The Essendon Football Club and its supporters: He

acknowledged the challenging period for the club but expressed gratitude for the fans' support during his seven years there, 2013 to 2020.

He thanked the Brisbane Lions and former Fitzroy supporters for embracing him and allowing him to "have a kick and stuff up a bit on the field."

He said he would keep his personal thanks to those close to him when the "dust settled." No doubt that included a special catch-up with Chris Fagan.

JOE DANIHER

Joe Daniher won a Crichton Medal and All-Australian selection in 2017, as well as the 2017 AFL Mark of the Year and Anzac Medal in that season

He was four times Essendon's leading goalkicker in his seven years at the club before being traded to Brisbane in 2021. Twice, he was the Lions' leading goalkicker. At the end of the 2024 season, with a premiership medal to his name, he announced his retirement, with a year still to run on his contract. He was 30 years old.

He played 108 games for Essendon, scoring 191 goals. At Brisbane, his 96 games produced 204 goals.

Daniher was drafted by Essendon from the Calder Cannons TAC team under the father-son rule, with the tenth overall selection in the 2012 national draft. He was also eligible to be drafted by Sydney, but chose to join the Bombers, where his brother Darcy was playing at the time. He made his debut against Carlton in Round 11.

Joe's father, Anthony, along with his uncles Terry, Neal and Chris all came from a family in Ungarie in NSW and played VFL/AFL football.

In 2018, scans revealed Joe Daniher had early onset of osteitis pubis (a non-infectious inflammation of the pubic symphysis causing varying degrees of lower abdominal and pelvic pain), causing him to miss the rest of the season after Round 7.

He suffered a calf injury that costs him several games in 2019 and at the end of the season, he requested a trade to Sydney but Sydney could not meet Essendon's terms and he played on in 2020.

After the 2020 season, exercising his rights as a free agent, Daniher moved to the Brisbane Lions.

Loyalty has been a big factor in Chris Fagan's career.

At the demise of the Reserves competition at the end of 1999, Fagan remained at Melbourne as an assistant coach until the end of 2004. He was offered a place in football administration, courtesy of newly-appointed Hawthorn coach Alastair Clarkson.

Clarkson and Fagan had become good friends while they were at Melbourne in the late-90s, and Clarkson sought him out to become his General Manager of Football Operations.

Fagan initially declined the offer, reluctant to desert Melbourne coach Neale Daniher who had given him his break in AFL football. Daniher's sacking by Melbourne in mid-2007 created the opportunity for Fagan to move on. In 2008 Fagan joined Clarkson at Hawthorn, as Director of Coaching.

He remained there until the opening arose at the Brisbane Lions in 2016-17.

The selection panel that chose Fagan as the Lions coach, saw in him genuine care for the game and players.

Former player Simon Black, the 2002 Brownlow medallist,

former Lions assistant coach and panellist for interviewing prospective coaches for the Lions in 2016 said: "I was part of the environment when it was at its lowest and I was also fortunate to be a part of the coaching selection panel and when Fages walked through the door, within 10 minutes, I was like, 'This bloke has got to be our coach.'

"It was almost like I didn't care how much he knew about the game, but his manner and his authenticity and genuine care that you could feel from him, it exuded from him.

"And I know he's had his knockers at times in the media with the strategic part of the game, but what he's brought – I mean, 80 per cent of our list is from interstate and if you don't have a great environment, they go home – so he's brought a real family type environment to the place and that's invaluable and that's been the foundation to build on to become the premiership club."

Black summing up: "He's just so authentic... you could just sense that he cared about the player and the human being more than the football and the game, first and foremost.

"He came from football management at Hawthorn for 10 years, but you just felt good about him. He had empathy. He had the ability to want to get to know the players. And we've seen that with the way kids get drafted. He's all over the country wanting to get to know the family."

Early in 2016 the strong media speculation was that Fagan would get the Lions job as he was known as a "stickler for high standards and a strong culture," just what many thought the Lions had lacked.

Sam Mitchell – who became coach of the Hawks in 2021 after the departure of Alistair Clarkson – touted Fagan as the best choice for the Lions. At that time Mitchell was a four-times premiership player with Hawthorn, a former captain and a Brownlow Medallist.

Speaking on radio station SEN in September 2016, Mitchell said that when Fagan spoke, people listened and that coupled with his ability to get the best out of others made him an asset.

"I'm not an expert in this (coaching appointments) by any stretch but all I can talk of is Chris Fagan himself and he is outstanding, he has great strengths. He would be genuinely good with the people.

"He sits in on all our leadership meetings. He's on the computer and doesn't say too much, he sort of takes the minutes and makes sure we're on track but when he does say something, usually it's something that no one ever questions it. It's usually a great idea. That ability to know what to do and when will certainly hold him in good stead.

"As far as the tactical stuff, he'll have to have other coaches around him like every coach does but his ability to bring people together and get the best out of people and that stability I think would be outstanding for any organisation. Although, I hope he doesn't get it because we would love to keep him at Hawthorn."

David Noble joined the Lions in 2016 as general manager of football after a decade at the Adelaide crows and was just in time to take part in the selection of a new coach.

Noble said at the time the senior coaching position in the modern game required more than just on-field strategy. It also required the ability to manage people.

"It's a very big role these days," Noble said when he arrived at Brisbane. "It's a senior exec role because you are managing a group of staff and a bunch of athletes at the same time.

"The role is about leadership, strong personal values, an ability to teach and educate and someone with good technical acumen."

He could easily have been talking about Fagan. Perhaps he was, as Fagan got the job. And Fagan got premierships.

Chris Fagan's willingness to contribute to the betterment of others sometimes takes him away from football.

He recorded a video in 2024: "The first thing I would say is, 'Have confidence in yourselves'. You made it into the final for a reason – because you were good. So respect your opposition, but don't fear them.

"The second thing is, move on quickly from mistakes. You will make them for sure tomorrow, but... be like goldfish and let them go."

That wasn't his address to the Brisbane Lions players on the eve on the 2024 Grand Final, but it could easily have been.

It was in fact part of a video-talk Fagan prepared for the Melbourne Girls Grammar debating team as they prepared for the C Grade Victorian State Debating Final against Camberwell Grammar in 2024, a month after the Lions won the AFL Grand Final.

Fagan was on holiday when he was approached by the school to help out. He had no direct connection to the school but was happy to oblige with a recording that set out some key points for the students.

"I think it was the old schoolteacher coming out in me," Fagan said. "My wife was egging me on as well.

"I just thought, 'Oh well, if it helps them, why not'. I think they came from nowhere, and they were the underdogs, a bit like us (The Lions in 2024), so I just gave them a few key points."

Just as the Lions did, the girls won.

They held up the winner's shield and recorded a message for the Lions coach: "Thanks, Fages."

Mental health advocacy also is an interest of Fagan. As senior coach, he has implemented practices to support players' emotional well-being, emphasising the importance of balance and the reduction of stigma around mental health challenges.

He has spoken about the importance of players studying or being involved in activities beyond football to appreciate life more fully – an holistic view of well-being. He has some thoughts on how to go about that.

"You need to get to know them as a person, what makes them tick, what motivates them – that's a key pillar," he says, "You have to create a supportive environment where people have the opportunity to grow and develop and thrive.

"To do that you've got to make it safe. Safety means they feel respected, can have an opinion... if they don't feel supported, they'll feel fear and trepidation and uncertainty, and that can get in the way of progress. That doesn't mean we create a warm, fuzzy environment where we all hug each other and sing Kumbaya. It's about honesty.

"I'd rather be a transformational coach, somebody who can coach the all-round athlete and help them develop as a person, as opposed to a transactional coach who just is interested in what you can do and what you play on the weekend."

Fagan supports the FightMND charity, which raises awareness and funds for motor neurone disease research, particularly in honour of his friend and former colleague Neale Daniher from his days at the Melbourne Demons. He has taken part in such events as the "Big Freeze" at the MCG, where football identities slide into ice-cold water to raise money for the cause.

That's the kind of person he is.

In January 2025, Fagan was among 70 sports identities who put their name to a call for Prime Minster Albanese to hold a royal commission into antisemitism and terrorism in the wake of the horrifying shooting attack on a Jewish group at Bondi Beach in Sydney. He, and Lions three-peat coach and Board member Leigh Matthews, were among around 20 AFL players, former players and former and current coaches who signed up to a letter to the Prime Minister.

WEATHERING THE STORM

Racism remains an issue in the AFL, despite the settlement of a high-profile case brought against identities from the Hawthorn Football Club.

The racism saga was one of the most significant controversies in Australian sport, extending from 2022 to 2024 and involving allegations of racist and culturally unsafe treatment of indigenous players and their families at Hawthorn.

In 2022, players and former players made accusations against senior Hawthorn football department officials.

Two years later, the accusations made their way into a court hearing where those subject of them and named in court documents included Alastair Clarkson, former head coach; Chris Fagan, assistant coach during Clarkson's tenure; and Jason Burt, former player development manager.

Fagan, and the other Hawthorn identities – Clarkson and Burt – always strenuously denied the allegations first put to them in detail just before Christmas 2022.

Two years later, and after two days of mediation before a scheduled Federal Court hearing, former Hawthorn players, their partners and the club agreed to a settlement.

The club and players issued a joint-statement confirming an agreement was met. The statement specified the settlement was reached "without determination of any parties' allegations."

Hawthorn issued an apology to the former players, their partners and their families: "Hawthorn accepts that the allegations were made in good faith, and has heard, respects, and accepts that they represent their truths.

"Hawthorn is sorry and apologises that the former players, partners, and their families, in either pursuing a football career, or in supporting such a person, experienced ongoing hurt and distress in their time at the Club."

End of story as far as racism is concerned?

No. In 2025 AFL CEO Andrew Dillon said combating racism was a continuing task.

"It's a societal issue and we're a part of society," he told the ABC, "It's not comfortable at all and doesn't really sit well with me. It's something that we want to work on."

The evidence of the extent of racism issues was plain to see.

In July 2025, St Kilda's Nasiah Wanganeen-Milera and Port Adelaide's Jase Burgoyne received racially abusive social media messages, related to football and possibly bets that had been made on matches by the likely senders.

Dillon: "It would appear there is still more work to do, and we know that and we acknowledge that. And that is something the AFL can't fix by itself. It's something that it's the AFL, it's our clubs, it's our players, it's our coaches... it's an all-of-industry approach that we are going to need to continue to make our environments the best they can be for all the men and women that play the game."

Players subjected to racism abuse can exercise their right to have it dealt with.

There is no telling what real toll the racism row that engulfed the Hawthorn Football Club over two years might have taken on Chris Fagan, or indeed any of those at the centre of the controversy.

At the time, Fagan paid tribute to his family and the Lions football club for providing invaluable support.

"It's challenging, but I've got a good family and a good footy club around me, so I've had plenty of support from them so I'm going OK," Fagan said after a big win against the Bulldogs in Melbourne in June 2024 as the sage drew on.

He said his support network made it easier for him to do his job "all the way through" after the allegations first surfaced.

"I'm very, very grateful to everyone that's close to me and some good mentors like Danny Daly and Phil Smyth. They've been pretty good to me too," Fagan said.

The controversy saw Fagan take a leave of absence from the club at the end of the 2022 season, and he watched his players celebrate the year at the best-and-fairest night in his tracksuit pants from home.

And when he needed to go for his usual daily stroll to deal with some of the considerable stress, Fagan would wait until night, unsure how others may react to the allegations and headlines.

"I went through a period where I was just at home and I wouldn't really venture out in daylight hours," Fagan told Melbourne's *Herald Sun*.

"I love my exercise and my walks, but, yeah, I would wait until it got dark every night to go for a walk instead. People don't know the truth, and people can take sides and I thought if I put myself out here what's it going to be like? Are people going to come up and abuse me?

"After a couple of weeks I realised I couldn't keep living like that. So I got back to normal and discovered that I didn't think I had a person say a bad word about me."

Fagan must have been relieved that the matter was eventually settled without adverse findings against him. Yet the absence of any clear statement in the announcement of the settlement in reference to Fagan and the other two former officials would have been disappointing.

An investigation by the AFL found in May 2023 there was no basis for adverse findings against the three officials, none of whom were still at Hawthorn by the time the case settled 18 months later.

ROLLERCOASTER OF EMOTIONS

A Brisbane club statement in 2022 vowed support for Chris Fagan as the unfolding Hawthorn racism saga engulfed several people, including the Lions coach from his time at the Hawks.

The statement said: "Since Chris Fagan arrived at the Brisbane Lions in October 2016, he has been more than just our Head Coach. He has been a role model, a mentor, and a father figure."

To those close to the Lions – fans, players and officials – it was a sentiment well expressed.

Few people, perhaps not even Fagan himself, knew the club's support of him, personally, was going to be more important in the years that followed.

After all, reaching the Grand Final in 2023 and winning it in 2024 painted a picture of a coach and his team in a happy place.

The Lions' thumping of Sydney by 60 points at the MCG for his first premiership victory always will remain a highlight of Fagan's football career.

He was living every football coach's dream. At 64, he'd just become the oldest coach in AFL history to win a premiership. But for almost four months after clasping his AFL premiership medal in September 2024, Chris Fagan battled some demons.

Coaches are not often thought of in the same way as players in their experience of health issues, particularly mental ones. They are seen to be above that, incorrectly as it turns out.

The cloud of the Hawthorn racism saga hung over those named, including Fagan, for two-and-a-half years until it was settled in November 2024.

As if the dragged-out Hawthorn racism saga wasn't enough to challenge his wellbeing, Fagan had faced another test of his resilience.

He had undergone tests for prostate and bladder cancer. And his mental health worried him.

For a brief time early in the 2024 season he thought about taking time out amid the stresses he was dealing with.

Club officials Andrew Wellington and Greg Swan, reportedly alerted by club doctor Paul McConnell, went to Fagan's home on 6 May to check on him and to talk things through.

Fagan later cited the visit as pivotal in helping him deal with the pressures and realise that he needed to re-focus on his coaching role.

Family support also was important.

"Blokes don't talk about this stuff nearly enough and they should," Fagan said at the time.

He was given the 'all-clear' on the cancer scare after a week of uncertainty and returned to the business of winning his first Grand Final.

But after the end of the 2024 season there was another health cloud. He confided in an interview with Channel 7 in September 2025, that he went through something of a rollercoaster of emotions.

"After we won the Grand Final, (I was) incredibly happy and (am) still incredibly happy and (it) will be one of the highlights of my life," Fagan told *Unfiltered*, a program that features conversations with notable people and goes "behind the scenes," often to highlight personal stories.

He discussed his experience over the three to four months after the Grand Final and into 2025.

"Not every day was good," he said.

He found the right support, working with the Lions' sports psychologist to manage his condition. "I had good people around me," he said. "I spoke to our sports psychologist. It was just everything mounted up, I think. And I was just physically, mentally exhausted.

"You know, again, we talk about mental health, but there's been the odd occasion in my life where panic attacks have come along, and they came along again after that Grand Final (2024) for probably that period of time (three to four months). Not every day; some days were good, but some days I'd wake up and think, how am I going to be today?"

It is not too difficult to work out what stresses Chris Fagan was going through. The racism saga and the health scare were obvious ones.

And there was football itself. He had taken a team that won the wooden spoon in 2017 to a Grand Final just six years later only to fall short of glory by just four points.

Getting his team back to its best after such a disappointment would take an almost superhuman effort. But he did it, and in 2024 the Lions gave Chris Fagan his first AFL premiership and the club its first for two decades.

Panic attacks are not rare. According to health authorities, around 40 per cent of Australians have a panic attack once or twice in their lives.

Someone having a panic attack, gets a sudden sense of overwhelming panic and fear.

Symptoms include extreme anxiety and physical sensations of fear, such as increased heart rate, shortness of breath, trembling and muscle tension.

Triggers can include over-breathing, long periods of stress, activities that lead to intense physical reactions (for example exercise, excessive coffee-drinking) and physical changes after illness or a sudden change of environment. Not all of those applied in Chris Fagan's case of course, and with the support of those close to him he was able to overcome the demons to steer the club to another permiership.

Chris Fagan's courage to talk about his experience should have gone a long way to help reduce the stigma around such episodes for many people.

It also explains his empathy with his players, a deep understanding of, and care for, their individual needs and experiences.

Of concern to Chris Fagan was the hubbub over Christmas 2025 and into 2026 surrounding star player Lachie Neale.

Club chairman Andrew Wellington has said Fagan "consistently prioritised the well-being of our players and staff" and worked hard to ensure a "culturally safe environment" for players and their families.

The Neale episode must have been particularly troubling to the coach. It wasn't his place – or in his nature – to talk publicly about it of course.

Wellington had described Fagan as a "tremendous ally for all our players and their families."

Amid swirling gossip and speculation fuelled by social media posts. Neale, turning 33 and joining the 300-games club in 2026, told teammates in the first week of January 2026, just before the squad resumed training, that he was stepping down as co-captain.

Neale shared the captaincy with Harris Andrews for three seasons after replacing Dayne Zorko at the start of 2023.

"Given the personal matters that I am currently working through, I have made the decision to stand down as co-captain and from the leadership group, effective immediately," Neale said on 2 January, "Having been a leader and captain of the Lions has been an honour, but it's time for the club to move forward with a fresh start.

"I spoke through this with the club over the last week or two with Danny (Daly) and with Fages (Chris Fagan), and it was a pretty easy decision for me, and time to move on and let someone else or Harris do the job by himself."

Reports were that Neale had discussed the co-captaincy with Fagan many months previously in the context of bringing new leaders forward.

Now though, circumstances gave the issue currency. Neale's welfare was of prime concern.

Lions General Manager, Football, Danny Daly: "Our priority as a football Club is to always support our people and their families. "We've been doing this privately with both Lachie and (wife) Jules during this difficult time. We do ask that their privacy and that of their children and families is respected at this time."

Neale referred to his marriage breakdown when he addressed the media: "While I won't go into specifics... I have let my family down. I apologise for my actions, which have hurt those closest to me, and for that, I am deeply sorry. I accept the consequences of my actions, and I need to focus on rebuilding that trust with Jules.

"I'm extremely disappointed in myself, and I've put plans and measures in place to do the work on myself so I can be the best version of myself moving forward."

The Lions have always emphasised privacy amid family considerations, the club often asking for respect for players' personal lives. Neale requested privacy as he moved forward.

How would Neale face up to the season amid all that had happened? That no doubt would be something to which Chris Fagan would have to turn his attention.

Neale would become a free agent at the end of the 2026 season, able to consider offers from other clubs, with keeping access to his children a likely priority in any decision.

A return to Western Australia in 2027 could be an option. Jules Neale originally was from WA. The couple were married in 2018. The Neales have two children – a four-year-old daughter, and a year-old son.

Chris Fagan said the club would not stand in his way if Neale wanted to return to WA.

FROM GRAVEL TO GLORY

Chris (Christian) Fagan, a timeline.

For the two-times AFL premiership coach, it has been a long road to the top from the Gravel Oval in Queenstown, Tasmania, to back-to-back Brisbane Lions' Premiership Cups on the MCG.

But the rewards for the man who started his working life as a schoolteacher have been well worth his football journey.

Born: 23 June 1961, Queenstown, Tasmania. Family moved to Hobart when he was a teenager.

Parents: Austin (died 2019) and Beth. Austin was a noted player and coach with the Smelters, Lyell and Gormanston Football Clubs.

Siblings: Grant, David and Anne-Marie. (Grant has coached Tasmanian team Clarence to five premierships).

Early years: As a youngster at Murray High School in Queenstown, a career in mining was an option – his father was an electrician at the Mt Lyell copper mine. A high school teacher saw his potential and Chris Fagan went on to the University of Tasmania and became a primary school teacher.

Wife: Ursula (they met at university and she also became a teacher).

Children: Two daughters, Jessica and Ellen (one is a teacher).

Occupations: Teacher (Batchelor of Education) for 12 years, then football coach.
Junior football: Learned the game on the Gravel Oval in Queenstown where, as a 15-year-old, he came to notice playing for Lyell-Gormanston. Loss of skin on the gravel surface was a rite of passage.
VFL team followed: Richmond.
First senior football: Joined TFL side Hobart in 1978 and represented Tasmania at the U17 Teal Cup in Adelaide.
Early notice: One of Tasmania's best players in the Teal Cup, he was invited to trial with VFL club Essendon. Essendon didn't recruit him and he stayed in Tasmania.
First influence: His father, Austin.

PLAYING CAREER

263 senior games in the Tasmanian State League, including Hobart, Sandy Bay, Devonport and representative games in Under 17s Teal Cup and State teams.
95 games for Hobart, 1978-82;
96 games for Sandy Bay, 1983-87 (former captain);
38 games for Devonport, 1988-89;
17 games for North Hobart, 1990;
Hobart TFL premiership, 1980;
Devonport TFL Statewide League premiership, 1988;
Hobart Best and Fairest, 1981;
Sandy Bay Best and Fairest, 1985;
Sandy Bay Leading Goalkicker 1983 (51), 1984 (34), 1985 (50);
9 representative games for Tasmania, 1981-86;
Tasmanian Teal Cup (U17s) representative, 1978.

REPRESENTATIVE FOOTBALL

Fagan represented Tasmania 11 times.
He played for Tasmania in national competitions in 1982-83. A competition conducted by the National Football League (NFL) began in 1976 as the NFL night series and comprised club-based teams from the Victorian Football League (VFL), West Australian Football League (WAFL) and the South Australian National Football League (SANFL), and combined sides from Tasmania, New South Wales, Australian Capital Territory and Queensland.

COACHING CAREER

He started his coaching career as an assistant to former Geelong hard-man Mark Yeates at North Hobart in 1991.

He spent two years as an assistant coach at North Hobart before being appointed senior coach of Sandy Bay for 1993 and 1994. He was the inaugural coach of the Tassie Mariners (Under 18s) from 1995 to 1997.

North Hobart Assistant Coach, 1991-92 (Premierships 1991-92);
Sandy Bay senior coach, 1993-94 (39 Games: 18 Wins, 21 Losses);
Tassie Mariners inaugural coach (national U18 – TAC Cup), 1995-97;
Melbourne AFL reserves coach, 1998-99 (44 Games: 30 Wins, 13 Losses, 1 Draw);
Melbourne assistant coach, 2000-04 (AFL Grand Final, 2000);
Melbourne General Manager Football Operations, 2005-07;
Hawthorn Head of Coaching and Development, 2008-13;
Hawthorn General Manager of Football Operations, 2013-16;
Brisbane Lions Senior coach, current to end of 2027 (216 Games: 129 Wins, 85 Losses, 2 draws);

Finals record: 20 games, 12 wins, 8 losses;
He coached his 200th senior AFL game on 24 May 2025, ending a five-game hoodoo against Hawthorn with a 33-point win at the MCG.

ADMINISTRATION CAREER

Melbourne General Manager of Football Operations, 2005-07;
Hawthorn Head of Coaching and Development, 2008-13;
Hawthorn General Manager of Football Operations, 2013-16.

Melbourne Demons senior coach Neale Daniher picked him for a job as Melbourne Reserves coach in 1998. "Finding Chris Fagan was the best recruiting decision I made in all my time at Melbourne," Daniher once said.

Fagan became assistant coach at Melbourne under Daniher from 1999 to 2007. The club reached the 2000 AFL Grand Final, losing to Essendon.

Fagan moved to Hawthorn Football Club as assistant coach and general manager of football (2008–16). The club won premierships in 2008, 2013, 2014 and 2015. He was head of coaching and development between 2008 and mid-2013. He was general manager of football to senior coach Alastair Clarkson between mid-2013 and the end of the 2016 season.

He was appointed head coach of the Brisbane Lions on 4 October 2016, succeeding former player Justin Leppitsch.

WITH THE LIONS

Fagan took the Lions to the AFL finals in his third year (2019) winning 16 games (six losses) after just five wins and 17 losses in his first two years.

The 2023 season was his best in terms of matches won, although it did not include a premiership. He produced 17 wins (six losses) and a narrow 4-point loss to Collingwood in the Grand Final.

His first AFL premiership came in 2024 with a 60-point thrashing of premiership favourites the Sydney Swans. The Lions won 14 home-and-away games in the premiership year, the least number since Fagan's second year, 2018 (the 2020 season was shortened due to Covid restrictions, and the Lions won 14 games and lost three).

Fagan followed up with his second premiership in 2025. The Lions finished third in the home-and-away series of 23 games with 16 wins, six losses and a draw.

AFTER A LOSS

"There's no point trying to talk to me after we lose, I am too lost in working out how we can do it better next time" – Chris Fagan.

MAKING PROGRESS

Fagan's first year at Brisbane was 2017. The previous year the Lions had won just three games and the numbers showed just how inept they'd been: 79 more goals conceded than any other team that year.

The glory days of the three-in-a-row premiership years (2002-03) were a distant memory, but dreams of another three-peat were revived in 2025 when the Lions won their second successive premiership.

CLUB HISTORY

The Fitzroy Football Club was formed at a meeting at the Brunswick Hotel on 26 September 1883.

The Victorian Football Association (VFA) allowed Fitzroy to join as the seventh club in 1884, playing in the maroon and blue colours of the local Normanby Junior Football Club.

In 1897, Fitzroy was a foundation member of the breakaway Victorian Football League (VFL).

The club was known as the Maroons until 1938, Gorillas (1938-57) and the Lions from 1957 when the maroon, blue and gold colours were adopted.

Fitzroy was one of the most successful clubs over the league's early years, winning premierships in 1898, 1899, 1904, 1905, 1913, 1916, 1922, and 1944, but a drought of success followed. Financial troubles through the 1980s and 1990s, saw the club placed into administration in 1996.

The newly created Brisbane Bears (playing out of the Gold Coast from 1986) also were struggling (70 wins, 148 losses, and 2 draws in 10 seasons) and only made their first finals appearance in 1995.

With a merger with Fitzroy, the Bears became the Brisbane Lions on 4 July 1996.

The Lions finished eighth in 1997, squeaking into the finals but progressing no further. They finished last in 1998.

Leigh Matthews, fresh from a premiership with Collingwood, was appointed coach towards the end of 1999 and the Lions reached the finals. A year later they were in the finals again, bowing out in the second week.

Then came the three-in-a-row and a runners-up under

Matthews, before another lean period, and a succession of coaches from 2008 onwards after Matthews moved on – John Blakey, Michael Voss, Mark Harvey and Justin Leppitsch had been in charge before Chris Fagan arrived in 2016.

In 2017 and 2018, the Lions won just five games in each season, with a drastically improved percentage from 2017 to 2018. In 2017 they were above average in total marks and fourth in centre clearances. They were top of the league average for total clearances.

In 2018, there was more progress. Despite again just winning five games, the Lions were fifth in clearances, second in marks, and just about broke even in the inside-50 differential.

The breakout year was 2019. The Lions went from five to 16 wins, only to lose in straight-sets in the finals, but at least their supporters had something to be pleased out – a finals appearance.

In 2020, they won their first final under Fagan. In 2021, they were in the finals again, but lost in straight-sets.

They won two finals in 2022 and in 2023 reached the Grand Final. The loss to Collingwood was heartbreaking.

Redemption was coming – the 2024 Grand Final saw the Lions dispose of the Sydney Swans in no uncertain manner. Victory was complete: the Lions had 80 more disposals, 70 more marks, and they won the inside-50s and contested ball stats.

Since 2019, the Lions were not lower than sixth in inside-50s, fifth for the marks differential, and third for clearances.

HOME-AND-AWAY RECORD (2017–25)

196 matches for 117 wins, 2 draw, 77 losses – 59.69%.

LIONS IN THE FINALS (2017-25)

The Lions played 20 finals matches 2019-2025 under Fagan for 12 wins (including two Grand Finals) and eight losses (including 2023 Grand Final) – 60% success rate.

100th GAME AS A COACH

Lions v North Melbourne, Hobart, Saturday 19 June 2021 (moved from Melbourne due to Covid restrictions). The Lions prevailed 9.14-68 to 6.9-45 on a wet and cold evening. Chris Fagan: "It was "one of those nights when you have to slog it out."

200th GAME AS A COACH

Lions v Hawthorn, MCG, Saturday 24 May 2025. ending a five-game hoodoo against the Hawks.
Lions won 14.9-93 to 8.12-60

REDEMPTION AT THE DOUBLE

Three times, Fagan's Lions bowed out of the September play-offs in games that were decided by less than a goal: the 2019 Semi-Final, 2021 Semi-Final and 2023 Grand Final. Finishing the home-and-away series fourth on the AFL ladder in 2024, the Lions went into the finals series as underdogs. After 14 rounds of the season, they were 13th on the ladder with several players injured. They reached the September finals series but few pundits gave them a chance of winning the premiership, particularly over the Sydney Swans who had been the dominant team.

The Lions had some close calls on the way to the Grand Final. Twice they were staring at defeat, but they came back.

First, they accounted for Carlton 99-71 at the Gabba. Then

they scraped home against GWS at Engie Stadium 105-100, earning a place in the preliminary final against Geelong. The Lions prevailed 95-85 in a match in which they trailed by 25 points at one stage during the third quarter.

On to the Grand Final, and the rest, as they say, is history: The Lions doubled Sydney's score in a blowout, 120-60.

"My phone went mad after the Grand Final and most of those were from friends and family in Tasmania," Fagan said.

The road to the Grand Final in 2025 was a little more straightforward. The Lions finshed third to secure a double-chance that they needed after losing the prreliminary final to Geelong. They then had to win a semi-final (Gold Coast) and prelimiary final (Collingwood) to earn a re-match against Geelong for the premiership.

Fagan commented: "The last three weeks we have played the best footy we have all year. They're just an amazing group that keep on keeping on."

CHRIS FAGAN'S HONOURS AND AWARDS

Playing

TANFL premiership player (Hobart): 1980.

TFL Statewide League premiership player (Devonport): 1988.

From his Tasmanian Football Hall of Fame Legend citation in 2023:

"A talented footballer in his own right, Chris represented Tasmania at the 1978 Teal Cup competition in Adelaide aged 16 and was subsequently invited to have a trial match with Essendon. Although the VFL dream didn't work out, Fagan was nevertheless destined for big things in football and joined

TANFL club Hobart in 1978. Over five seasons and 130 games Fagan's impact at the Tigers as a fine rover/forward pocket was significant, playing in the 1980 premiership, winning the Best and Fairest the following season and representing his state for the first of 12 occasions.

"In 1983 he joined Sandy Bay and spent five years with the Seagulls, claiming a Best and Fairest there too as well as three consecutive club goalkicking awards. After his work as a teacher saw him transferred to Sheffield in 1988, Fagan continued his career with Devonport, playing a key role in their 1988 Statewide League premiership before retiring after one final season with North Hobart after more than 250 senior games."

Coaching

AFL Coaches Association Allan Jeans Senior Coach of the Year Award: 2019, 2024, 2025. He is the first coach to win the award three times in it's 22 -year history.

BUILDING A DYNASTY

As many families were thinking about their 2025 Christmas as December arrived, the Brisbane Lions launched their pre-season at Brighton Homes Arena on the first day of the month.

The senior players were there, along with some youngsters just starting out on their careers.

There was some star quality present – new Australian athletics sensation Gout Gout was among the guests.

Premiership defender Harris Andrews was impressed by the sprinter: "He does a bit of stuff in the kick room and that sort of thing, its very impressive to see how explosive he is.... He's a pretty unbelievable athlete."

The 2026 season promised much, by way of a dynasty and even a three-peat of premierships, not that either of those things was front-of-mind for the players.

Andrews said the Lions couldn't afford to be tempted to get carried away by the possibility of a three-peat.

"Certainly not looking that far ahead, I think for us now, we'll just break down the pre-season block by block," Andrews said at the pre-season launch.

Most players had already begun work, including the new arrivals, despite the arrival of the Queensland summer, with daytime temperatures from 28-30 degrees.

There were gaps to be filled in the Lions squad at the end of the 2025 season – premiership players Ah Che and Starcevich had moved on and McInerney had retired. Replacing like-with-like was a challenge.

However, captain Harris Andrews believed the club wouldn't be fazed by the exits, thanks to off-season recruitment and the club's philosophy.

"You're always evolving as a footy club," Andrews said at the Lions launch, "To lose Starcevich, Ah Chee and McInerney, we'll miss those guys, but we had a fair bit of changeover the year before as well. We're not naïve, guys will move on, but we'll get new players in as well. It's next man up."

The much-vaunted Lions midfield weas intact – Neale, McCluggage, Dunkley and the Ashcrofts were still on board.

The trading period and Draft proved vital in filling gaps and providing depth.

Trading places

The AFL player trading period in 2025 was described as one of the most dramatic – club captains and superstars of the game found new homes and some clubs refused to release players who wanted to be traded.

The *Herald Sun* newspaper noted that the "balance of power" in the AFL seemed to have switched to the Queensland clubs, John Ralph writing: "Brisbane getting stronger ahead of its three-peat campaign with the salary cap space for Sam Draper (ex-Essendon), Oscar Allen (ex-West Coast) and the re-signing of dual Norm Smith Medallist Will Ashcroft."

Ralph said of the Gold Coast: "Gold Coast landed game-changer Christian Petracca and took the game's biggest risk in

Jamarra Ugle-Hagan," and "Gold Coast finally making waves in a manner that should put it firmly in the premiership race."

Brisbane also secured its top priority in the 2025 Draft – Daniel Annabel, a Lions Academy player rated in the top half dozen prospects.

Draper and Allen were recruited as free agents in the trading period. Getting Sam Draper from Essendon looked like a big plus after the retirement of Oscar McInnerny. However, a foot injury to Draper pre-season meant he would likely miss several games.

Landing Oscar Allen (former West Coast captain and key forward) would hopefully fill a gap left since 2024 when Joe Daniher retired and again in 2025 when Callum Ah Che went off to Adelaide.

There are two types of free agents – restricted and unrestricted. Unrestricted free agents have served eight years or more at one club, are out of contract, and can automatically move to the club of their choice. There is no need for a trade. It includes any player that has been delisted.

Restricted free agents have served eight years or more with one club and are in the top 25 per cent of wage earners at that club. They can receive offers from other clubs. If the offer is matched – both in duration and financially – by their current club but the player still wants to move, a trade then has to be arranged.

The Lions were in a good position after the 2025 AFL free agency period. They lost two-time premiership defender Brandon Starcevich to the West Coast Eagles but gained two established top-quality players (Allen and Draper).

One concern on the horizon for the Lions was that there

could be free agent issues at the end of 2026. Forward Zac Bailey, originally from South Australia, would likely face interest from Adelaide and Port Adelaide. Some reports said his management had before the end of 2025 fielded offers exceeding $1.3 million per year from rivals. Essendon was known to be keen on getting him.

The 26-year-old was born in Darwin but went to school in Adelaide and was selected out of Norwood in the SANFL in the 2017 Draft. He signed a two-year extension in 2023 to take him to the end of 2026.

The Lions probably would need a long-term extension to keep him.

The Lions could also face interstate interest in Lachie Neale who would be 33 at the end of the 2026 season and also become a free agent without a contract extension. Two West Australian clubs inquired in 2025 of Neale's possible availability but were given short shrift. The West Coast Eagles saw him as a possible mentor for their young players.

He, too, would be worth a contract extension at Brisbane for his leadership if nothing else. But by staying at Brisbane has become less likely amid his family issues.

Neale arrived at Brisbane on a five-year contract at the end of 2018 after seven years at the Dockers. He was signed for an extra three years at the end of 2023.

At the start of the 2026 season he needed just six games to reach 300.

After the 2025 season, the Lions delisted 4 players: Darcy Craven, Deven Robertson, Brandon Ryan (who will look for other clubs) and Lincoln McCarthy whom the Lions reinstated to their list through the rookie draft.

Clubs with vacant list spots were able to add players to their list any time between the draft and the start of the competition in a supplemental selection period and West Coast, which had four rookie list spots granted by the AFL, picked up Robertson. Fremantle picked up de-listed Collingwood big man Mason Cox.

The Lions were well aware of the need to carefully manage their salary cap, known as TPP (total player payment), as well as bolstering specific areas of their team structure. The recent departures of McStay, Daniher and Starcevich – and the move back to South Australia of Ah Chee in the pre-season draft – would have eased some of the salary-cap pressure.

McInerney, Ah Che and Starcevich were key players leaving the 2025 premiership line-up. Replacing them required the club's full attention.

Adding a key forward (Allen) and a ruckman (Draper) to the list was significant. A slight concern was that both were coming off injuries that ended their last season.

Both had serious injuries in 2025, Allen limited to 12 games, and Draper five.

The Lions didn't seem concerned about Allen's injury record and offered him a long-term contract.

As with every trading negotiation, medical checks are involved and the Lions were happy to have the pair on board.

They would have been aware of what happened with Dan Hanneberry's expensive switch from the Swans to St Kilda in 2019.

Four seasons later, in August 2022, Hanneberry's run of injuries forced him into retirement after just 17 games with the

Saints. He was 31 years old then. Allen still had youth on his side – he was 27 when the 2026 season started.

Fagan observed as training began: "They are really energetic blokes, and I love those sorts of players in our club.

"Both are great characters; they both have a sense of fun. They've both been in leadership roles at their club, which is great because we lost a little bit of leadership with Starce (Brandon Starcevich) going back to Perth, and Oscar McInerney (retired) was in our leadership group,

"I think Draper was regarded very highly at Essendon for his leadership abilities and the way he can bring fun to the place.

"It's good to have those two players... we thought they might take a little bit longer, but they are back, albeit a little bit modified."

Allen seemed a good prospect for a leadership role, having been captain at the Eagles. He said it got to the stage in the West where the offer to leave was greater than the offer to stay. And the Lions had made him feel "wanted."

He said: "I get to go to a situation where I know that I'm really wanted, they've put all these things in front of me and been really clear that they wanted me. So, that's a great feeling for me as a person, for someone to really want to have you there, so that for me was great. Why wouldn't I want to go somewhere where everyone really wants to have me here?"

Brisbane couldn't get a satisfactory deal done to grant Callum Ah Chee his wish to be traded to Adelaide, and he had to nominate for the pre-season draft where he got his wish. The Lions received nothing for the move.

During the trading period, the Lions sought a first-round

pick in return for letting Ah Chee go, which the Crows rejected. Brisbane knocked back an offer of a future second and a future third-round pick, leaving Ah Chee in football's limbo.

Lions list manager Dom Ambrogio said the club "put a number of options to the Crows," and said the deal could have been reached in different ways "but at the end of the day (Adelaide) chose to put forward the offer they chose, and it didn't meet our needs."

Ah Chee's manager Ben Williams: "We're disappointed in Brisbane. You're talking about a 28-year-old dual-premiership player. We tried to go through the front door and be as transparent as possible and the deal hasn't been done."

Having finally secured a return to the team he'd always admired and despite the premiership success he enjoyed, Ah Chee commented: "It was a really strange situation, but I understand that footy at the end of the day is a business and the reality of it is these things can happen.

"It's been a little bit tough with the uncertainty of it all, but I had faith it would all get sorted out and we would end up where we are today.

"I'm finally happy to have closure now and move. I'm super thankful to the Brisbane Lions for everything they did for me and so appreciative of the past six years."

Ah Chee was drafted by the Gold Coast with their first selection and eighth overall in the 2015 national draft. He was traded to Brisbane at the end of the 2019 AFL season.

His departure from the Lions could be covered by Eric Hipwood and a recovered Lincoln McCarthy.

Covering the departure of Starcevich had implications for the defensive unit.

Jaspa Fletcher was thought likely to take on a senior role in defence, possibly in cahoots with Jarrod Berry. Both had shoulder surgery, but the club saw they had the potential to step up.

Fox Footy pundits summed up Brisbane's outlook for 2026 as positive.

Leigh Montagna: "They're in Seat 1A going into 2026. They want for nothing. They've brought in Draper and Oscar Allen and they'll bring in a top-five draft pick, potentially, with the academy pick (Daniel Annable) – and they're in the box seat. It's only going to be motivation or injuries that will really slow them down next year. They didn't really need to do much. They do lose Starcevich, who will be a big out with his ability to shut down the best small-medium forwards in the competition, will be missed. But they've got enough depth there to be able to cover that."

David King: "They are the envy of the competition. You look at the guys who've played 50 to 80 games – that's where the real growth comes from – now they're establishing themselves, there's confidence in their body and what they can do gameday ... they've got an unbelievable window in front of them. It's exciting if you're a Brisbane fan."

Jon Ralph, *Herald Sun*: "To think Brisbane could be on the brink of a second three-peat this century ... who would doubt a team that won 16 home-and-away games despite the AFL's toughest fixture and who won their flag despite losing the qualifying final?"

To most fans, the annual trading period remains mystical.

It is complicated, and there is little point trying to explain how draft picks are determined, how players are rated and how compensation picks work, and so on. The swapping of draft picks gets confusing as the picks can extend as far forward as two seasons.

The main excitement is generated by knowing which players were leaving and arriving for the next season.

The 27-year-old Draper signed a five-year deal with Brisbane and would be the replacement in Brisbane's ruck division for recently retired Oscar McInerney.

In the case of the 26-year-old Allen, West Coast chose not to match Brisbane's six-year contract offer worth around $900,000 per season.

Allen was West Coast's co-captain and leading goalkicker in 2023. He would be an ideal scoring prospect, something Brisbane had been looking for since Joe Daniher's retirement at the end of 2024.

The Ashcroft brothers signed contract extensions to take them through the next five years – Levi, 18, for an extra three years from 2027 and Norm Medallist Will, 21, also to 2030. Levi said extending his contract was a "no-brainer" in the success the club was enjoying. He played very game in his debut season. Defender Ryan Lester was playing on in 2026 after signing a new one-year deal.

Chris Fagan described the 2025 AFL trading period as an extension of the club's "long-term plan" to remain a premiership contender while integrating new talent for sustained success.

The recent acquisitions and the draft capital accumulated through trades (Brisbane held nine draft picks going into the

2025 selections) was part of the club's strategy – not just reacting to "win-now" needs, but looking ahead three or four years.

Fagan acknowledged that letting go of Brandon Starcevich was tough, but stressed the importance of refreshing the list and giving opportunities to rising stars.

Starcevich had been a key part of the back-six and had a decisive role in shutting down Patrick Dangerfield and Tom Papley in the last two grand finals. Brisbane's other best small defender, Noah Answerth, was going to miss the start of the 2026 season after rupturing an Achilles. On the up-side, Keidean Coleman was expected back on the track.

Brisbane's list management team was "brave and smart" in their trading and drafting, and Fagan credited the club for staying focused despite speculation and outside pressure.

He said the playing group was still "hungry, humble, and ready to challenge again."

The 2025 trading period was in contrast to 2024 as far as the Lions were concerned. They were far less active in the 2024 trade and draft periods than in previous years. They didn't make any major mature-age signings, opting to focus on accumulating draft assets and mid-draft picks and swaps. The strategy centred on boosting the club's draft hand for the future.

Sam Day joined the Lions from the Gold Coast via the 2024 pre-season draft, playing 13 games in 2024 before retiring at the end of the season.

Harry Sharp was the only departure, traded to Melbourne where he played 18 games in 2025 after being drafted by Brisbane in 2021 and playing 16 games.

The years just before and immediately after Fagan's arrival at the Brisbane Lions were unspectacular to say the least.

But Chris Fagan was to change everything.

Here was a brand-new senior coach with new ideas and a focus on building a culture in which players, particularly younger ones, felt comfortable. He gained a reputation as someone who cared for his players and built strong relationships with them.

Were the recent dual premiership successes of Fagan's Lions more to do with how the AFL draft worked or the "new" culture at the club? Fagan spoke about the club's culture when he gave a presentation to the AFL commission after the 2025 Grand Final.

Amid calls from some quarters for the scrapping of father-son priorities and access to academy players via AFL drafts, Fagan told the commission the success of the Lions was down to an improved club environment and a culture under which players flourished. Players wanted to be there.

There is no doubt the Lions had done well under both draft processes, but Fagan pointed out that the noise seemed to be coming from clubs which hadn't had success via the draft options that were available.

He detailed the club's progress in all areas and gave commissioners a written summary that included a comparison of academy picks which showed the Lions had done no better numbers-wise than Gold Coast, Essendon, North Melbourne, Richmond and St Kilda through 2024 and 2025.

As for the father-son rule, Fagan said he was "amused" by the criticism. He believed the loudest critics were clubs that "don't have any father-sons at the moment."

"I'm not sure if they would be coming out with the same complaints if they had a handful. And what goes around comes around. I mean, Brisbane didn't have any father-sons not so long ago, and it's just happened that we've popped up with the two Ashcrofts (Will and Levi) and Jaspa Fletcher.

"But it might be a long time before another player or two comes along, and it will be someone else's turn."

He called the opportunity for sons and daughters of former greats to play for the same club a special and important part of the game. He was "in no hurry" to see the rule changed. Fagan said his club's success stemmed from culture and development, not unfair access to talent.

After four years in the bottom four, including a "wooden spoon," Fagan still had a massive challenge. His first year in change didn't change much that was obvious outside the club.

But his coaching style appeared to have had a profound impact, particularly on recruitment decisions. His experience as a teacher in in other football clubs would be vital in developing the young players. A move to the Lions became an attractive proposition for experienced elite players and emerging talent.

The club's focus switched to key positions and role players. The recruitment of Luke Hodge and Charlie Cameron was a sign the Lions were heading in the right direction, Fagan said in 2017, his first year at the helm.

Hodge had planned to retire but he had a long-standing association with Fagan, Hawthorn's former football chief, and the Hawks agreed to trade him to Brisbane for draft pick No.75.

Fagan said at the time: "We're trying to become a great club, and part of that is attracting great talent to our football club. I'm sure (the Hodge trade) will send a message across the competition that Brisbane's a good club to come to and, hopefully, others in time will follow in his way.

Just as big a coup for the Lions was the recruitment at the same time of Charlie Cameron from Adelaide. Here was a young player wanting to join the club rather than leave it as had been the case with others in previous years.

"And obviously with Charlie Cameron coming on board... that's a great boost to our club," Fagan had said.

It was hoped the acquisition of Hodge and Cameron would help the development of youngsters Hugh McCluggage, Jarrod Berry and Eric Hipwood.

Hodge, 33 at the time he joined the Lions, said: "One thing Fages has mentioned is that he wants me to go and help the younger guys but, also at times, maybe take a few games off to see how they handle it and who wants to take that next step."

The idea paid off, in spades.

Fagan and recruiting manager Stephen Conole went on the road to welcome the new recruits in 2017.

Cedric Cox and Alex Witherden joined McCluggage and Berry in a more youthful-looking Lions line-up in 2017, with key roles for the older-wiser heads as well.

Fagan played a direct role in welcoming and integrating new recruits, including Hodge and Cameron, presenting draftees with their team kit and attending press conferences with his new players, typical of his hands-on coaching philosophy Lions fans were seeing for the first time.

Charlie Cameron (from Adelaide, 2017 trade period, first played for Brisbane in 2018) became a premier small forward and All-Australian, central to Brisbane's forward line resurgence.

The Lions were astute in their recruiting over the five years from 2018. Lachie Neale followed Cameron and Hodge to Brisbane and became the master of the midfield.

Lincoln McCarthy (2018) developed into a valuable forward option. Jarryd Lyons (from Gold Coast for 2019) added some consistency around the ball in the midfield. Lyons retired from football in 2025 after a year with SANFL team Glenelg.

Probably the most significant acquisition was key forward Joe Daniher (from Essendon as a free agent for 2021). Daniher retired after the 2024 Grand Final.

Darcy Fort (from Geelong for 2022) was recruited as a ruck/forward. Conor McKenna (returned to AFL from Ireland in 2023) was installed as a half-back. Jack Gunston (from Hawthorn for 2023) was an experienced forward brought in to add scoring options but after one season went back to Hawthorn.

The Lions didn't overlook good young players during that period. Cameron Rayner (No. 1 pick in the 2017 draft, debut 2018) became a powerful forward/midfielder.

Zac Bailey (2017 draft) became a versatile midfielder/forward. Noah Answerth (2018) became a valuable and flexible defender. Kai Lohmann and Darcy Wilmot (early 2020s drafts) were important players as the Lions continued to build their list. And of course, father-son picks Will Ashcroft and Jaspa Fletcher (drafted late 2022 for the 2023 season) have become highly rated midfielders, preparing to follow Neale into the established core of the team.

The youthful face of the Lions prospects heading into 2026 featured the Ashcrofts, Wilmot, Fletcher, Morris and Kai Lohmann, all under 23.

The newly recruited Allen and Draper wasted no time

settling in. In November 2025 they joined the guard of honour by the men's team for the Lions' AFLW team for their preliminary final against Carlton (the Lions won by 35 points to meet North Melbourne in the Grand Final, losing to the Kangaroos side that was unbeaten all season.)

Some of Chris Fagan's Lions returned to the training track near the end of November in hot conditions with Allen and Draper on board.

It was an early return to work for the premiers, Hugh McCluggage noting the efforts of the newcomers: "You're such a close group you're keen to get out there and get to work, Oscar Allen and Sammy Draper, really throwing themselves into it.

"It's awesome to see the way they've attacked it. It gives us confidence, but a lot has to go right to get back to where you have to get back to."

Feeling the draft

Able to match Richmond's Pick 6 bid for their Academy product Daniel Annabel, the Lions got their man. He will be an important addition to their midfield armory.

The Lions didn't have a top-15 pick but held 1,756 draft points, enough to secure the 18-year-old Annable, rated by AFL Talent Ambassador Kevin Sheehan as one of the top midfield prospects.

Sheehan's assessment: "A hard-working midfielder/forward, Annable used his strong work rate and contested ball-winning ability to impact games. Has produced dominant performances for three years at both underage and VFL levels. Was a star for the Allies in the National Championships this year, particularly against both South Australia and Western Australia. He averaged 24.8 disposals, 4.3 clearances and 3.8 tackles across four matches to win selection in the All Australian Team. His selection topped off a great underage career after earlier in the year captaining the Australia U18 team in a match against Richmond's VFL side, where he won the best-player medal. Annable handled the step up to VFL level comfortably with the Brisbane Lions, averaging 21.3 disposals in eight matches... rounded off his year with a top ten finish in the 2km time at the national Draft Combine with a time of 6:21."

Put him in a side with Josh Dunkley, Hugh McCluggage, Lachie Neale, Jarrod Berry, and the Ashcroft brothers; what midfield talent the Lions would have! Even add Dayne Zorko, Cam Rayner, and Jaspa Fletcher as required.

How would that not still be the best midfield in the AFL?

For Annabel, being drafted by the Lions was a dream come true.

"I grew up barracking for the Lions, so I've always had such a passion and love for the club and to be able to get the opportunity to play for them is unreal and something my family and I will truly cherish," he said.

"Playing VFL for the Lions this year (2025), I saw the Club's culture first-hand and how they genuinely value each other's company and make everyone feel comfortable – it's a culture that I want to be a part of."

Annabel is a realist. He recognised that he may not go straight into the midfield, that he may be pushed out, maybe to another position.

"That wing role, that high forward role, similar to what Levi did this year, is something I can see myself doing. I'm open to playing anywhere, being really versatile and have a growth mindset," he said after he was confirmed as a Lion.

He is willing to bide his time before a start in the senior side.

"'It's definitely going to be a goal coming into the year but there's no expectations," Annable said, "I'm extremely ready, I've started off-season training already so I'm excited to get to know the boys a bit more and meet the coaches and the staff as well.

"Whether I play Round 1 or Round 10, it doesn't really matter. I know I've put the work in, and I'll continue to do that.

"The VFL games I played have helped heaps and the experiences I got were invaluable. The leadership group in the VFL have been very good at making me feel comfortable and helping me get to know the group a bit better. So it's unreal. I'm going to a back-to-back premiership club; there's no better place to be. It's a club I have so much love and passion for, just as a fan, so I'm excited to finally be joining them and get to work."

While Annable is seen as a strong contender for senior games, Fagan recognises that he may need to start his AFL career in more versatile positions such as wing or half-forward, similar to the way Levi Ashcroft made his mark before moving to the midfield full-time.

Annable is physically and mentally prepared, but his immediate opportunities will depend on how well he adapts to different roles and the team's needs throughout the season.

Annabel was presented with his Lions jumper (No. 18) by retiring ruckman Oscar McInenery.

Annable, a graduate of the Brisbane Lions Academy, grew up in Queensland playing for Redland-Victoria Point.

The 18-year-old had an impressive underage career at all levels as well as finishing in the top 10 for the 2km time trial at the National Draft Combine (a series of physical tests designed to assess the athletic capabilities of prospective AFL players.)

The 184-centimetre midfielder starred for the Allies in the National Championships where he averaged 24.8 disposals, 4.3 clearances and 3.8 tackles.

He also averaged 21.3 disposals for the Lions at VFL level.

Not just a talented player, he has leadership potential and was captain of the Lions Academy and the Under-18 All Australian team.

Lions National Recruiting Manager Stephen Conole said the Club was thrilled to have secured Annable.

"Dan is a terrific, contests player, a clean ball handler and has shown he can impact games when pushing forward as well.

"We look forward to seeing his development as a Lion."

The recruitment of Annabel complements the Lions' successful 2024 draft that secured Levi Ashcroft and Sam Marshall, previously a teammate of Ashcroft with the Sandringham Dragons. Both joined the Lions which matched first bids from Melbourne and Sydney respectively.

The Lions also had fellow Academy members Isaac Waller, Harrison Bridge and Tyan Prindable available for the 2025 draft.

Prindable, touted as a midfield star, was drafted by Collingwood with pick 32.

Waller and Bridge, also rated as top prospects and members of the Allies team in the Under 18 championships, were not drafted and will bide their time.

Academies are important recruiting grounds for AFL clubs.

Looking to the 2026 draft, two Brisbane academy prospects stood out: Cooper Hodge, son of four-time Hawthorn premiership player Luke, making him also father-son eligible for the Hawks, and Maroochydore lad Caylen Murray, who previously was named in the All Australian Under16 team.

Concessions for Academy players that have already paid off for the Lions include Harris Andrews (2025 premiership co-captain), Eric Hipwood, Jack Payne and Keidan Coleman.

To the end of the 2025 season Andrews had played 239 games since graduating through the Northern Academy system.

The Northern Academy comprises talent development programs established by the four clubs north of Victoria – Brisbane Lions, Gold Coast Suns, Sydney Swans, and Greater Western Sydney Giants – to nurture junior Australian Rules footballers in those states.

Also, each AFL club has a designated region where it runs a Next Generation Academy (NGA) program aimed at ages 11-18, focusing on Indigenous and multicultural youth who may have less access to traditional football pathways. Activities include football skills clinics, leadership and teamwork programs, fitness and training sessions, and education in areas such as cultural awareness and healthy living.

The AFL's draft is in two main parts, the national draft and the pre-season draft and are held in successive weeks before year's end.

The National Draft is mostly how clubs add players to their lists, specially among school-leavers and others who are eligible.

The pre-season draft, held after the national draft and before the next season, is for uncontracted players who missed the national draft or were delisted.

There is also a rookie draft which has been at the centre of some debate about its purpose and use.

Instead of exclusively being used for actual rookies, clubs are using the mechanism to move players around their list.

Brisbane used the rookie draft to re-recruit Lincoln McCarthy after delisting him.

Another pathway into the AFL used by the Lions – and other clubs – is via Gaelic football.

Each club can include up to three extra players (referred to as Category B rookies) on its Rookie List provided the player either:

- has not registered in an Australian Football competition for three years immediately before inclusion on the Rookie List;
- is an international player, not an Australian citizen and has not lived in Australia for a substantial period;
- is a former NSW Scholarship player with that club;
- is a former International Scholarship player with that club;
- is a rookie Zone Selection for clubs based in NSW or Queensland.

Irish players can be signed under the International Player Rule and do not have to go through the draft.

Clubs can now list one Irish player as a Category B rookie.

The Lions in 2025 signed teenage star Ben Murphy as the third Irishman to play for the club.

Murphy, an 18-year-old from Kerry, signed as a Category B rookie and joins as a defender, but the club believes he could play other positions.

Lions scout Shane Rogers: "He has been a midfielder in

Gaelic, though with his size and athletic profile it should allow him to play multiple roles.

"He will start as a defender while he learns the game but has scope to develop his craft across a number of lines and the ability to play wing long term.

"He stands at 191 centimetres and is growing, he has speed, has agility and an ability to read the game quickly.

"One of the attractive aspects of his recruitment is his calm demeanour, especially when under pressure within the game that allows him to make excellent decisions."

Murphy joins countrymen Conor McKenna and Darragh Joyce at the Lions.

McKenna has played 49 games for Brisbane (and 79 for Essendon), including the Lions' triumphant Grand Final in 2024. He also played in the losing decider in 2023, but didn't win selection for the 2025 Grand Final.

"It's great to re-sign for 2026 and I'm really looking to another big season," the 29-year-old said. "I've loved my three years at the club so far, both on and off the field, which made it an easy decision to stay on."

Joyce has played 13 games for the Lions since arriving from St Kilda in 2023. "It feels great to re-sign because it is amazing just to be part of this special group," he said, "I love the group, love the boys and rocking up to the club every day, so it was an easy decision to re-sign as I am not ready to give up those locker room vibes just yet. As a club we would love to get back to the finals again and personally I would love to get a taste of that too."

Lions general manager of football Danny Daly: "Both

Conor and Darragh continue to work hard, and their new contract is due reward for their effort. They are determined to put in a solid pre-season and continue to push for AFL selection in 2026 which we look forward to." (The club also has three Irishwomen on their AFLW list; Neasa Dooley, Jen Dunne and Orla O'Dwyer).

Irish players are confident they can adapt to the AFL.

"AFL is similar enough to Gaelic, though I expect to face a few obstacles like getting used to a totally new ball – but I'm excited to face the challenge," Murphy said.

"There have been a number of players make the switch like Conor and Darragh already at the club. But there are also a few other players that I aspire to be like... Mark O'Connor, Cillian Burke (Geelong) and I went to school with Rob Monahan (Carlton) as well.

The Lions re-signed Irish pair Conor McKenna and Darragh Joyce on one-year deals for 2026.

Lincoln McCarthy was reinstated to the Lions' list in the rookie draft. He spent 2025 recovering from a second knee reconstruction after rupturing his anterior cruciate ligament (ACL) on the eve of the season.

After joining from Geelong at the end of 2018, McCarthy played 122 games for Brisbane before his first knee injury in May 2024. He played only eight games in 2024 and suffered the second rupture at a training session in March 2025.

Delisted players can explore moves as free agents. Deven Robertson, for example, was on the radar of the West Coast Eagles. He turned down an offer to join the Eagles and move home at the end of 2023 but his opportunities in the Lions midfield were limited after the recruitment of Will and Levi Ashcroft, and Jaspa Fletcher.

The youngsters who would take the Lions into 2026 and beyond: Will Ashcroft, Jaspa Fletcher and Darcy Wilmot (21); Levi Ashcroft (18), Ty Gallop (19) Logan Morris (20) and Kai Lohmann (22). Another key player still with youth on his side would be Cam Rayner (25).

Emerging youngsters James Tunstill and Luke Beecken were re-signed for 2026. Tunstill, a midfielder originally from Western Australia, played 12 games since being drafted in 2021.

Beecken, who made his AFL debut in the Lions' win over Fremantle in Round 23 in 2025, joined the Club via the mid-season rookie draft in 2023. A SANFL premiership player, he had performed well at VFL level, providing dash off half-back with ability to break lines. Keeping the 2025-26 squad together might prove problematic.

One piece of the puzzle was solved just before Christmas 2025 when former draftee Darcy Wilmot, now 21, extended his contract from 2027 to 2029. A key defender for the Lions, he had three Grand Finals under his belt, won two premierships and made 14 finals appearances in his 83-game career. The Lions drafted him at Pick 16 in 2021.

Head of football Danny Daly: "We knew when we drafted him that he had plenty of ability and potential, and to his credit and our coaching staff he has developed into a top defender.

"Darcy has been a key player in helping us experience success and we look forward to many more years of having him, his partner Dion and their families at the Club."

Originally from Victoria, Wilmot said he hadn't dreamed of

playing anywhere else.

"This place, I'm so comfortable with the city, the players, the staff... I'm so happy here," he said.

"We all move (from interstate) and this is like you're family away from family and that's the culture that's been built here."

Brisbane was definitely a destination club.

The cost of retaining the emerging players eventually would increase as would interest in them from other clubs. There is no doubt Chris Fagan made the Lions a destination club but what would the future hold if he enacted his contract expiry in 2027?

Going into the draft period, Fagan had emphasised the need for balance between adding fresh talent – such as highly rated draft prospects – to fortify the list depth, while also ensuring the team did not lose its competitive edge.

For Fagan, the 2025 draft was a strategic opportunity to bolster the Lions' list while nurturing the next generation of club leaders and stars.

The Lions' successful navigation of the 2025 off-season strengthened their status as premiership contenders for 2026, with a mix of proven star recruits and elite young talent.

Betting is a sore point in sport, but for what it is worth betting agencies opened up with the Lions at favourites ($4.60 to $5) for the 2026 premiership (just over $1 for the top 10). Gold Coast and Hawthorn at the end of 2025 were on the second line at $8.

TRUE BELIEVERS

'There were times, even up until last year when we won the flag, I felt maybe there was a little bit of impostor syndrome. I feel (now) like maybe I do belong in the coaching ranks.'

Chris Fagan, 29 September 2025

Lions players and fans were thinking three-peat as the 2026 AFL season approached.

Chris Fagan was talking about a "dynasty."

Foxfooty.com.au posed the question: "Has there been a team better placed for a dynasty?"

The seeds of the Fagan dynasty were there: thumping wins in the 2024 and 2025 Grand Finals. Followed by some astute recruiting.

The Lions already had a three-peat in their history; Leigh Matthews' players did it in 2001-2003.

A three-peat has only been achieved six times in V/AFL history, and only the Melbourne Demons have achieved it twice.

Recruits Draper and Allen when at their best form would give Brisbane's "talls" an imposing look, possibly the best in the league, according to some commentary.

The main thing to worry about – and it is always a factor for any team – would be a devastating run of injuries to key players.

The Lions had survived 2025, after season-ending injuries

to Noah Answerth, Keidan Coleman, Eric Hipwood, Tom Doedee, Lincoln McCarthy and Jack Payne. Lachie Neale late in the season looked like missing the Grand Final but recovered to take a place on the Lions' bench then contribute to their premiership victory.

Coleman and McCarthy each both missed almost two seasons.

When the shouting and the tumult died down after the 2025 premiership, this was the reality of the Lions' rise to the top:

Since 2018, no club had won more games than the Lions. The least number of wins in every season had been 15. They'd contested every finals series and could easily had had three premierships (two would have to suffice at the end of 2025). They'd won more finals games than any other team.

As preparations for the 2026 season stepped up, the Lions looked in good shape.

Josh Dunkley and Kai Lohmann had surgery on their injuries, Eric Hipwood, Noah Answerth and Jack Payne were all in rehab through the 2024-25 summer and Keidan Coleman was looking forward to a solid pre-season build-up after two seasons of injury battles. Unfortunately, Hipwood seemed unlikely to reappear until mid-way through the season.

Another factor the Lions were wary of was improvement among the premiership challengers. Hawthorn for example had the makings of another premiership dynasty. Geelong and Collingwood, though somewhat humiliated in 2025, would be expected to be near the top of the ladder again.

Several teams showed promise in 2025, but couldn't get to

the "big dance" – Adelaide, GWS Giants and Fremantle among them. They could be contenders again in 2026.

The Swans couldn't do what the Lions did after a Grand Final loss; after losing in 2023 by the narrowest of margins, the Lions came back bigger and better.

Blown away by the Lions in 2024, the Swans could manage only 10th a year later. They were thought capable of fighting back after their 2024 disaster but couldn't mount a serious challenge a year later.

Demoralised? To be fair, a new coach might need a couple of seasons to get make them a threat again.

And how about this for a longshot? An all Queensland Grand Final. The Gold Goast Suns showed in 2025 they could contend in finals. They showed glimpses of what they'd be capable of in 2025, and have added Christian Petracca to their line-up. Their home record is strong, too.

Were the Lions really capable of a three-peat?

AFL pundits and betting agencies thought so, as clubs started sorting out their playing lists for 2026.

Replicating the efforts of the 2001-03 triple premiership side was always going to be a talking point inside and outside the club. Discussion was inevitable.

Midfielder Hugh McCluggage explained: "When you get there (to a grand final) it's exciting but you don't want anyone else to taste it, you get selfish.

"The night of the grand final... it's honestly just the happiest night.

"The smiles, the pure joy, the adrenaline.

"You lap it up for a little bit, but yesterday you're doing laps in 38 degrees and you're back down to earth pretty quickly."

A three-peat to reprise the Matthews era?

"We're our own team, taken a different journey to get there but you've got the fans saying why can't we?" McCluggage said.

The Lions didn't want to get carried away with such thoughts, no matter what the fans were hoping for.

McCluggage: "As soon as your mind goes too far forward it falls apart pretty quickly."

Brisbane's midfield was widely considered the best in the League. Their forward line would be bolstered by the arrival from the West Coast Eagles of Oscar Allen; they had a squad of young players who would only improve; and the defence line was skilled at suffocating the attack of opponents.

The Lions got by with four main goal-scoring options in 2025, but only Logan Morris with 53 from his 26 games was in the top 10 scorers (8th). Joe Dainher led the way the previous season with 58 goals from 27 games.

In 2025, six teams had players with 60 or more goals for the season, Geelong's Jeremy Cameron leading with 88. Would goal scoring be a weak link in 2026?

Going into the season, Logan Morris again shaped as the primary spearhead after leading Brisbane's goalkicking in 2025 with more than 50 goals. He'd established himself as the central target inside 50 metres. Oscar Allen was also a scoring option, having scored 50 in previous seasons with the under-performing West Coast Eagles.

Charlie Cameron was still one of Brisbane's most potent scorers, having been the club's leading goalkicker in multiple seasons previously, and averaging around a goal and a half per game in 2025. Cam Rayner and Zac Bailey also rank among the Lions' potential top goal contributors.

Midfielders Hugh McCluggage, Lachie Neale and Will Ashcroft also were capable of scoring from stoppages and forward-half contests.

It was a positive that the Lions had multiple scoring options.

According to the AFL pundits, key factors influencing the Lions' chance at a three-peat included:

- Squad depth and injury management, especially among younger players stepping into critical roles.
- Strategic innovation by the coaching staff to counter rivals' evolving tactics.
- The psychological resilience of leadership figures and star players under sustained pressure.
- Home-ground advantage at Brisbane Stadium, with its passionate crowd.
- Transfer period moves and draft picks shaping the final roster for 2026.

Lions List Manager Dom Ambrogio said the arrival of the two free agents (Allen and Draper) was exciting for the Club.

"To have secured Oscar and Sam (Draper) this trade period is a great result and we see both players really strengthening our list."

The Lions had youth on their side, too: Will Ashcroft, 21, a two-time Norm Smith Medal winner with just less than 60 games under his belt; Levi Ashcroft, 19; Logan Morris, 20; Darcy Wilmot, 21; Jaspa Fletcher, 21, and Kai Lohmann, 22.

From the 2025 premiership team, only Dayne Zorko, Ryan Lester, Lachie Neale, Darcy Fort, Charlie Cameron and Darcy

Gardiner were over 30. Yet, according to the statisticians, Brisbane's premiership side was the third oldest in the League. Go figure.

Collingwood holds the record for the most consecutive premierships with four in a row from 1927 to 1930. Hawthorn won three in a row from 2013 to 2015 after Brisbane's three-peat 2001-2003.

Two three-peats would be something amazing, although it could be argued (by Magpies supporters of course) that Collingwood's four in a row constituted two three-peats.

Understandably, Chris Fagan was optimistic about the Lions' prospects. He highlighted the depth of young talent in the squad, with rising stars such as Will Ashcroft and a group of eight players aged 22 or under primed to make significant contributions.

The club had re-signed important emerging players including James Tunstill, a promising midfielder, and Luke Beecken, a half-back who has already impressed at VFL and AFL level. Veteran Dayne Zorko, known for his leadership and performance across half-back, was also poised to play a key role and was set to post a record number of club appearances.

Changes to AFL rules for 2026 would impact how coaches managed their teams.

The move to a five-man bench was expected to make it easier for clubs to accommodate two ruckmen, something that could prove valuable with new rules providing for quicker re-starts after stoppages. The recruitment of Sam Draper would be a valuable acquisition for the Lions but Chris Fagan will have to manage him carefully via interchanges with other ruckmen in the squad as the season progressed. (Clubs would continue to have up to 75 rotations per game). Darcy Fort had been back-up ruckman to Oscar McInenery and would most likely have a similar role with Draper, having re-signed to the end of 2026. The early injury to Draper could mean academy prospect Isaac Waller, 18, could come into the picture for a rucking role, having been part of the Lions' Academy program since he was 12.

In 2026, ruck contest rules with a ball-up instead of a bounce at stoppages would likely favour leaping specialists, something the Lions would have had in mind when recruiting Draper.

At Essendon, Draper showed aggression, speed, competitiveness, sound follow-up work at ground level and physical presence in hit-out contests.

New AFL Executive General Manager Football Performance, Greg Swann (formerly at the Lions) acknowledged there had been a strong push for changes to the substitute and bench rules.

"It'll give coaches a little more flexibility, whether they play two ruckmen, for example, because they've got that extra person on the bench. We don't do everything in here on the basis of [whether] the clubs want it, but in this instance, there was a strong push for it," he said.

"Having come out from clubland, it was always difficult for the person who was the sub. In our case, in Brisbane, you'd be down as the sub, then you'd have to fly back to Brisbane and play in the VFL and all that sort of stuff. In this instance, we just thought it was a no-brainer."

A highly significant change to the AFL competition was announced late in 2025.

A wildcard round was introduced to the finals format, the league effectively becoming a top-10 finals system instead of top-eight.

On the weekend previously reserved as a pre-finals bye, the seventh-placed team at the end of the home-and-away season hosts the 10th team and the 8th team plays 9th in the two wildcard games. The top six teams have the weekend off.

The winners of the two wildcard games progress as part of a steeper five-week passage to the premiership for the teams who finish seventh and eighth.

Based on the 2025 ladder, a wildcard round would have seen Gold Coast play the Sydney Swans and Hawthorn play the Western Bulldogs.

The new format means each of the top-eight teams will all host a final in 2026.

Brisbane finished second in 2025 and a wildcard system would have had no direct bearing on their finals matches.

The Lions were hopeful of avoiding the wildcard round in 2026, and their form over recent years suggests that hope wouldn't be misplaced.

Analysts suggested Brisbane did reasonably well out of the 2026 home-and-away draw, rating their schedule as the 8th hardest, much more acceptable than 2025 which was probably the toughest. A downside was that they would only play two home-and-away games at the MCG, in Rounds 6 and 24.

The Lions were slated to face Sydney, Geelong, Essendon, Carlton, Gold Coast and Collingwood twice.

Lions Chief Executive Sam Graham said that as back-to-back Premiers, the club was looking forward to the 2026 season with multiple blockbusters scheduled for the Gabba.

"We're looking forward to seeing our fans pack out the Gabba again, the atmosphere and energy the crowd brings our team is like having another player on the field and we want the Gabba to remain our fortress," he said.

"Our home games are scheduled across a range of days and timeslots which gives flexibility to our growing fan base with six of our Gabba games against teams that finished in the Top 8 this season."

The Lions were to play six games in Victoria, and would host Collingwood, Adelaide, Carlton, Geelong, Fremantle, Sydney, Port Adelaide, Hawthorn and the Suns. With the Suns tipped by many to be the big improvers after a successful trade period and good prospects from their academy, the Q-derbies were likely to be "blockbusters".

A couple of other possible downsides – the Lions would be playing their South Australian Gather Round match in the Barossa Valley against North Melbourne. They would play more than half their matches on a Saturday, and they had few prime-time games.

What can fans expect to see in the seasons ahead? It almost certainly won't be "more of the same" as tactics will continue to evolve.

The Lions already had the best midfield, and that would continue to be a strength, even with some new faces involved.

Their defensive pack isn't bad either, with co-captain Harris Andrews pivotal to its prowess.

Harris Andrews was appointed captain for the Grand Final win over Geelong, a fitting reward for one of the best defenders in the League. Usually, he was co-captain with Lachie Neale who was on the bench for the first half.

Andrews, a two-time All Australian, Merritt-Murray Medal winner and Academy graduate, was ranked No.1 in the League in 2025 for spoils (163 for the season) and averaged three intercept marks and 13.3 disposals per game. In his four finals, Andrews averaged 9.75 intercepts.

He is a hard defender to get around – if he's not taking a defensive mark, he is punching the ball away from an attacking player.

Pundits rated Andrews, Dayne Zorko, Dary Wilmot and Darcy Gardiner in the top 10 defenders of the season, the accolade for Andrews backed up by Champion Data that ranked him as the League's No. 1 defender.

Andrews is contracted to the Brisbane Lions until the end of the 2029 AFL season. Fagan has consistently praised Andrews for his resilience and defensive leadership and success in 2026 may well turn on his star defender remaining at his inspirational best.

The Lions didn't have Keidean Coleman, Jack Payne, Noah Answorth and Tom Doedee for most of the 2025 season. Their return in 2026 was much anticipated and, hopefully, Jaspa Fletcher going into the mix. Ryan Lester, after being convinced by retired premiership winner Joe Daniher, agreed to extend his AFL career by at least one more season, his 16th at the elite level.

Longevity is not guaranteed on playing lists of course; contracts expire and players seek to move for a variety of reasons. As much as a club might want to keep a playing list together for as long as possible, the reality is that there will be movement each season.

Chris Fagan has emphasized the "amazing ride" the club has been on but warned against complacency.

He has often stressed that injuries and squad changes are opportunities for new players to step up. Expect this approach to continue, fostering a "next man up" culture and encouraging squad depth.

He wouldn't of course mention his personal contribution (investment might be a better word) towards the Lions' success.

Fagan noted that the Lions' resilience and emerging youth put them in an excellent position not just for 2026, but for the years ahead.

Brisbane almost certainly would be the only AFL club he would coach. He was staying put, having in 2024 signed a contract extension to the end of the 2027 season. He'd be 66 then.

With additional top prospects and key recruits joining for 2026, Fagan suggested the club could be at the start of a dynasty rather than nearing its end.

And it is worth noting his philosophy that premierships are won by squads rather than just the 23 named for game day.

The single word on the club banner as the Lions ran out for the 2025 Grand Final on the MCG seems apt: "BELIEVE".

CHRIS FAGAN: LEGEND

Tasmanian Football Hall of Fame inductee: 2014.
Tasmanian Hall of Fame Legend: 2023.

Citation: "Name almost any role within the sphere of football, and Chris Fagan has most likely mastered it. From the infamous 'Gravel' to the hallowed turf of the MCG and beyond, Fagan has carved out a career both on and off the field that very few can match for longevity or sustained excellence."

Chris's brother Grant also is a member of the Tasmanian Football Hall of Fame; he played for Sandy Bay then coached Clarence to five statewide league flags (he was assistant-coach to Stevie Wright in the Clarence Roos' 1993-94 premierships).

2025 Allan Jeans Senior Coach of the Year

2025 Neale Daniher Lifetime Achievement Award

The 2025 AFL Coaches Association Awards on the 2025 AFL Awards Night, included the AFLCA Allan Jeans Senior Coach of the Year award and the Neale Daniher Lifetime Achievement Award.

Chris Fagan was honoured with both awards, the third time for the Allan Jeans award and second in succession.

"It's a great honour to be voted by my peers as the Senior Coach of the Year," Fagan said.

"I'm part of a committed team of Coaches and support staff at the Lions who strive to deliver a high-quality program on a daily basis to bring out the best in our players.

"The energy and expertise that our coaches bring to their roles has been pivotal to our consistency and success as a team. I know it's my name that goes on the trophy, but in reality, it's the work of the coaching group that matters most and so I accept this award on behalf of everyone who works in our Football Department at the Lions.

"I also want to recognise and thank the players for their efforts. The main responsibility for performance sits on their shoulders. The players at the Lions are great characters and committed professionals who make our job as coaches so enjoyable and rewarding.

"The standard of the AFL competition continues to rise and much of this is due to the work of the coaches at every club. It's a positive that this has been recognised by the AFL, with increases in the soft cap going forward to next season. It's important that this trend continues into the future."

AFLCA CEO Alistair Nicholson: "'Fages has shown himself to be an inspiring leader for the Lions and it's not hard to see why he is so well respected by the coaching fraternity.

"It's great to see him earn this kind of recognition after a long journey and extraordinary commitment, over many years, to the coaching profession."

Chris Fagan polled a total of 305 total votes, securing the award ahead of Grand Final opponent Chris Scott (245 votes) and Adelaide's Matthew Nicks (128) who led his side from 15th on the ladder in 2024 to the minor premiership at the end of the home and away season.

The Grand Final victory wasn't included in the voting but

would only have further cemented Fagan's accolade as the Coach of the Year.

The criteria for receiving the Neale Daniher Lifetime Achievement Award in the AFL are based on an individual's exceptional and sustained contribution to Australian football throughout their career and recognises such attributes as playing, coaching, administration, and broader service to the sport.

The recipient must have a distinguished record of achievement and service spanning many years in the AFL or Australian football community.

Contributions may include significant accomplishments as a player, coach, mentor, administrator, or in a combination of these roles.

The recipient's work must have left an enduring, positive mark on the sport, its culture, or its community, often demonstrating leadership, innovation, and mentorship.

Candidates are chosen for their ability to create a lasting legacy both on and off the field, such as advancing the sport or inspiring others through advocacy or charitable work.

The award honours Neale Danaher's contributions as a player, coach and administrator, including his role in founding FightMND, an organisation dedicated to finding treatments and a cure for Motor Neuron Disease.

Previously named for John Kennedy, the award was renamed for Neale Daniher to recognises his legacy, on and off the field.

Daniher's career included significant achievements as a player, coach (he picked Chris Fagan as his assistant at Melbourne), and executive, but equally notable is his work for FightMND, raising millions for research into Motor Neurone

Disease and inspiring the broader football community.

Chris Fagan's citation highlighted his career in football, from player and coach back in Tasmania to his roles as administrator and coach in the AFL. It also recognised the many honours he had received, including induction into the Tasmanian Football Hall of Fame and Coach of the Year awards.

No doubt Fagan was honoured to receive the award, but his lifetime achievements were not done yet.

Decades from now, after he's put his feet up and he's watching football from a distance, Chris Fagan will be spoken of as a legendary coach of the Brisbane Lions.

There is little doubt he would be most deserving of official "Legend" status at the club.

Back-to-back premierships have sealed it. A three-peat will enhance the legend. His contract has him staying put until the end of 2027.

He has said little to indicate he would stay as coach beyond the end of his contract. He by then will be 66.

It is of course up to the club to bestow official "legend" status on anyone, but to fans, he will always be regarded as a legend.

Chris Fagan already has Legend status in his home state of Tasmania. A similar accolade at Brisbane would not surprise.

Consider what he achieved going into 2026.

Chris Fagan took over a wooden-spoon side at the end of 2016 and turned it into a regular finalist, reaching finals in 2019–22, then a narrow Grand Final loss in 2023.

Then came the flags – back-to-back premierships in 2024 and 2025, one of few non-playing coaches to win multiple flags and the oldest coach of a premiership team.

His accolades reach beyond the club. He is a three-time AFL Coaches Association Senior Coach of the Year (2019, 2024, 2025), the first person to win the award three times. He also has received a lifetime achievement honour from the Coaches' Association.

In mid-2025 he reached the coaching milestone of 200 games for Brisbane, the 46th AFL/VFL coach to do so and just the sixth current coach to do so.

That's impressive for someone who admitted he felt something of an imposter until his Lions won the premiership flag in 2024.

The Brisbane Lions Hall of Fame already recognises major coaches and figures from both the Fitzroy and Brisbane eras as "Legends".

Given Fagan's achievements in reviving the club, winning consecutive premierships and the respect he holds in the broader AFL community, when his coaching career is finished, Legend status awaits.

So far, most of the Lions "legends" are players from the triple premiership era at the start of the 21st century.

They include:

Michael Voss – Inspirational captain of the 2001–03 premierships, Brownlow Medallist, multiple Best and Fairest winner, and later senior coach, often regarded as the club's greatest player and on-field leader.

Simon Black – Elite midfielder, triple premiership player, Brownlow Medallist, Norm Smith Medallist, and multiple club Best and Fairest, widely viewed as one of the AFL's most complete on-ballers. He is regularly ranked No. 1 in "all-time Lions" lists.

Jason Akermanis – Dynamic, goal-kicking midfielder/forward, Brownlow Medallist and triple premiership player, remembered for match-winning brilliance including his decisive 2002 Grand Final goal. He has been a long-time fan favourite.

Nigel Lappin – Highly skilled two-way midfielder, four-time All-Australian and triple premiership player, renowned for his courage, including playing the 2003 Grand Final with broken ribs. Perhaps the most underrated star of that dominant midfield group.

Jonathan Brown – Power forward and later captain, triple premiership player, Coleman Medallist and multiple Best and Fairest, who became the club's key spearhead and spiritual leader after Voss. He was a forward to be feared.

It wouldn't be fair to focus only on the legends created in recent history. Fitzroy had its legends, too, long before the merger with Brisbane. Fitzroy champions remain important to the Lions' identity.

Kevin Murray – Fitzroy great and Brownlow Medallist, officially recognised as a "Legend" in the merged club's Hall of Fame, reflecting the club's commitment to honouring its pre-merger history.

Haydn Bunton – Triple Brownlow Medallist for Fitzroy, also elevated to "Legend" status in the Brisbane Lions Hall of Fame as one of the most decorated players associated with the club's lineage.

Garry Wilson – Fitzroy star midfielder and multiple Best and Fairest winner, also honoured as a club "Legend" for his influence in the 1970s and early 1980s.

These are current and newly retired players who may well become Legends:

Dayne Zorko – Long-serving midfielder/forward and captain in the 2010-20 era, consistently high in "all-time Lions" rankings with an impressive Best and Fairest tally and praised for his leadership during the club's rise back up the ladder.

Lachie Neale – Elite midfielder and multiple All-Australian, widely recognised as one of the competition's premier on-ballers. His individual honours and ball-winning ability place him among the club's top modern players.

Harris Andrews – Key defender and multiple All-Australian, often mentioned among the best intercept defenders in the league and a cornerstone of Brisbane's contemporary backline. His leadership in defence has been crucial during the club's return to contention.

It would only be fitting that their coach becomes a Lions Legend, too.

BRISBANE LIONS CLUB AWARDS 2025

Rookie of the Year: Levi Ashcroft
Marcus Ashcroft Most Professional Player Award: Hugh McCluggage
Shaun Hart Trademark Player of the Year: Josh Dunkley
Players' Player of the Year: Josh Dunkley
Finals Player Award: Harris Andrews
Youi Game Changer Award: Zac Bailey
Life Memberships: Greg Swann and Eric Hipwood

AFL AWARDS 2025

Jim Stynes Community Leadership Award (presented at the Brownlow Medal count): Lions co-captain Harris Andrews.

Andrews is a committed advocate for creating safer and more respectful communities and has been commended for his focus on empowering young people, particularly boys, to develop emotional intelligence and reject violence.

Since 2018, Andrews has been an active ambassador for Beyond DV, engaging directly with vulnerable youth and volunteering at events to support those impacted by domestic and family violence.

Playing a key role in the development and launch of the 'Ask a Mate' initiative, which is a prevention program promoting respectful relationships and consent education, his leadership helped to mobilise over 20 public figures and teammates to amplify the campaign's reach, including the launch of a dedicated app in 2025.

Andrews has devoted countless hours to helping others

through his ongoing involvement with Beyond DV, spending time at the organisation's Recovery Centre, driving fundraising efforts and leading community events to strengthen support for primary prevention efforts across Queensland.
AFLPA Most Courageous: Josh Dunkley

BRISBANE LIONS ALL AUSTRALIAN HONOURS 2025
Harris Andrews (defender): 2019, 2020 All Australian Team. 2018, 2023, 2024 Extended Squad. 23 matches in 2025, 0 goals, 1 behind. Averages 13.5 disposals, 89.1per cent disposal efficiency, 7.7 marks, 3.0 intercept marks, 7.3 spoils and 2.5 rebound 50s.
Hugh McCluggage: Never Previously All Australian team. 2019, 2020, 2021, 2022 Extended Squad. 23 matches, 13 goals, 12 behinds. Averages 27.0 disposals, 67.5 per cent disposal efficiency, 12.0 contested possessions, 5.8 clearances, 2.1 centre clearances, 4.7 tackles, 7.6 score involvements and 5.8 inside 50s.
Zac Bailey: Never Previously All Australian. 22 matches, 33 goals, 30 behinds. Averages 19.7 disposals, 72.3 per cent disposal efficiency, 4.7 marks, 3.4 inside 50s, 6.7 score involvements, 0.1 contested marks, 2.2 tackles and 0.6 goal assists.

2025 AFL Coaches Association Monjon Allan Jeans Senior Coach of the Year Award: Chris Fagan, second successive year.

The Brisbane Lions were awarded the McClelland Trophy in 2025 as club champions of the AFL. The trophy has been awarded annually since 2023 to the club with the best aggregate performance across the Australian Football League (AFL) and

AFL Women's (AFLW) seasons. It was until 2022 awarded to the AFL club with the best results across all grades but the admission into the AFL of interstate clubs which didn't field teams in all grades and the introduction of the AFLW brought about the change. The trophy carries a prize of $1 Million.

The Lions have contested seven ALFW Grand Finals including 2025 since the League's inception in 2017 and been premiers twice, losing the 2025 Grand Final to North Melbourne who were undefeated through the season.

QSport Awards

Queensland team of the Year. Accepting the award, Fagan paid tribute to his players and the wider Lions administration team.

"It's a great honour to be standing up here and representing the Brisbane Lions Footy Club on the back of winning two Premierships in a row," he said.

"It's pretty hard to do and takes a great team of people on and off the field to achieve it.

"It's always challenging, after you win a flag, everyone comes after you and I think our boys, this year, showed a lot of humble confidence and when we played in the big games this brought out the best in us.

"I feel like everybody at the club both on and off the field has earned this award.

"We've been a really good team now for about seven years, we've played in the last three Grand Finals and we hope we can do it again."

THE RISE OF THE LIONS

The Lions came into being in 1996 when AFL expansion club the Brisbane Bears, established in 1987, absorbed the AFL operations of one of the league's foundation clubs, Fitzroy, established in 1883. The club's colours of maroon, blue, and gold were drawn from both Fitzroy (originally the Maroons) and the Bears. The Bears club finished in the bottom three 11 times in the 1960s and 1970s, including three wooden spoons in four years between 1963 and 1966. The club won only a single game between 1963 and 1964 – known as the "Miracle Match" when it defeated eventual premiers Geelong in Round 10, 1963. Its 1964 season was winless (no draws either), and as of 2026 stands as the only winless season by any club since 1950.

The Brisbane Bears were born in 1987 and played home matches at Carrara Stadium on the Gold Coast. The club was uncompetitive and after the collapse of the business empire of Bears deputy chairman Christopher Skase and the resignation of chairman Paul Cronin, the club was taken over by the AFL and re-sold to Gold Coast hospitality businessman Reuben Pelerman. The Bears finished last in 1990 and 1991 and amid financial losses the club reverted to membership ownership and played games at the Gabba in Brisbane. Meanwhile Fitzroy also was in strife. AFL club presidents rejected a move to merge the club with North Melbourne. Eventually, Fitzroy was placed into administration, and its administrator accepted an offer to merge its AFL operations with Brisbane.

Fitzroy played its last VFL/AFL game on 1 September 1996 against Fremantle at Subiaco Oval, and the Bears' last match was a preliminary final on Saturday 21 September 1996 at the Melbourne Cricket Ground against North Melbourne.

The Brisbane Lions were officially launched on 1 November 1996, joining the national competition in 1997. The newly formed Brisbane Lions played their first AFL game against the Adelaide Crows on 29 March 1997 at the Gabba before 18,474 spectators. Adelaide 17.13 (115) defeated Brisbane Lions 11.13 (79).

Fitzroy: 8 senior VFA/VFL premierships: 1895 (VFA), 1898 (VFL), 1899 (VFL), 1904 (VFL), 1905 (VFL), 1913 (VFL), 1916 (VFL), 1944 (VFL)

Brisbane Lions: 5 senior AFL premierships.
2001, 2002, 2003, 2024, 2025

BRISBANE'S COACHES:

Bears: *1987-1989*: Peter Knights (59 games, 16 wins, 43 losses, 0 draws), *1989*: Paul Feltham (7-5-2-0), *1990*: Norm Dare (22-4-18-0), *1991-95*: Robert Walls (109-30-78-1), *1996*: John Northey: (25-17-7-1).

Lions: *1997-98*: John Northey (34 games, 12 wins, 21 losses, 1 draw), *1998*: Roger Merrett (11-3-7-1), *1999-2008*: Leigh Matthews (237-142-92-3), *2009-13*: Michael Voss (109-43-65-1), *2014-16*: Justin Leppitsch (66-14-52-0), *2017-current*: Chris Fagan (216-129-85-2).

Caretaker coaches: *2005*: John Blakey (one game, one loss) filled in for Leigh Matthews on bereavement leave.

2013: Mark Harvey (three games, 2 wins, 1 loss) replaced Michael Voss after his resignation.